YOU, TOO, CAN BE

Simple Steps To Personal, Social, and Spiritual Fulfillment
For All Ages

Marvin L. Smith, D.D.

ACKNOWLEDGEMENTS and CREDITS

Footnotes for this work have been omitted in order to save space. However, all quoted materials are acknowledged by the name of the writer or speaker.

All Scriptural references are listed by Book, chapter, and verse, along with the translator of record. And biographies from various sources have been credited to the copyright holder of material used.

The fore mentioned material can be found in the Bibliography located in the back matter.

I freely acknowledge and express my deep gratitude to those whose assistance was very necessary to get this book into print. They are:

Mrs. Ruby Nichols, who contributed information on youth needs and desires.

Mr. Eugene Kendall, whose article in the Oklahoman on American student attitudes is included.

Dr. Thomas E. English, who served as proofreader and editor for the book.

Mrs. Jerri Shepherd, who drew and furnished much of the artwork.

Mrs. Mamie A. Smith, my wife who has been very successful in correcting my many mistakes before allowing me to publish this work.

PREFACE

YOU, TOO, CAN BE SUCCESSFUL, is written as a guideline for attaining the success in life which you may have desired, but have never been able to fully accomplish.

I'm sure that many who **have arrived,** or at least, have discovered the secrets of abundant living, are no doubt more qualified than I to give advice to those who are still seeking.

Yet, my desire is to share with you some values which are aimed at achieving your goal of becoming a successful and fulfilled person.

I cannot claim to have completely arrived at this lofty goal of myself, [*if I have arrived at all*]. By studying wisdom of the Sages, by gaining some maturity through the experience of years of failure, but especially through humble submission to Christ my Saviour, it is possible that I have gained some insight and understanding which has been a great contribution to my life.

Therefore, this guide is a combination of steps which I have personally put to use, and also which others who seem highly successful and happy are living by each day.

Ultimately, **you must determine** the value of this work for yourself by putting it to **your personal test.** However, "nothing ventured, nothing gained." **Why not try it?** It might just be the information you need to make you a **successful and fulfilled individual** able to help others also.

Trust in the Lord with all thine heart; and lean not unto thine own understanding. In all thy ways acknowledge Him, and He shall direct thy paths.

[*Proverbs 3: 5, 6*]

— M.L. Smith

CONTENTS

**CHAPTER I.   YOU, TOO, CAN BE SUCCESSFUL!!!
WHETHER IN YOUTH, MIDDLE-AGE, OR OLD AGE** 1
   A. Young People From Puberty Into Young Adulthood 1
   B. Middle-aged? You, Too, Can Be successful 3
   C. Senior Citizen? You, Too, Can Be Successful 5
   D. Are You A Parent? You, Too, Can Be Successful 9

CHAPTER II.   PREPARING TO BE SUCCESSFUL 15
   A. Desire To Be Successful..........................16
   B. Observe Others Who Are Successful 17
   C. Success Relates To Happiness 18

CHAPTER III.   WORK TO BECOME SUCCESSFUL 25
   A. Research Your Subject For Success....................29
   B. Learn Your Subject For Success 31
   C. Seven Steps That Lead To Peak Performance...........35

   SUMMARY OF CHAPTERS I, II, and III 40

CHAPTER IV.   ATTITUDES CAN MAKE YOU SUCCESSFUL ...43
   A. Exercising Faith To Become Successful 45
   B. Exercising Hope To Become Successful 50
   C. Exercising Love To Become Successful 51

**CHAPTER V.   PRAYING THAT YOU WILL BECOME
SUCCESSFUL** 57
A. Prayer From The Human Point Of View 58
B. Prayer From The Divine Point Of View 60
C. Does God Always Answer Prayer? 64

**CHAPTER VI.   THE ASSURANCE OF BECOMING
SUCCESSFUL** 69
A. Youth In Junior High, Senior High, & College 70
B. Middle-aged Adults Are Concerned For Their Future 70
C. Many Senior Citizens Are Very Concerned 72
D. Parents Of Young Children Are Very Concerned 74
E. You Can Increase Your Mental Potential For Success . . .76

**CHAPTER VII.   HOW TO BE ASSURED OF BECOMING
SUCCESSFUL** 81
A. All People Want To Be Successful 81
B. Shoot For The Top Of The Success Ladder 82
C. Attainment Of Spiritual Values Are The Greatest
Assurance 86
D. Christians Are Always Successful!!! 88

SUMMARY OF CHAPTERS IV, V, VI, and VII 93

**CHAPTER VIII.   LOOKING AT OTHERS WHO BECOME
SUCCESSFUL** 99
A. Since Biblical Times 99
B. Some Successful People Whom We Have Personally
Known 102
C. Trust God To Get Your Career On The Right Tract 107
D. How To Know That You Are Successful!!! 109

— Notes —

CHAPTER I.

YOU, TOO, CAN BE SUCCESSFUL!!!
WHETHER IN YOUTH, MIDDLE AGE OR OLD AGE:

YOU ARE — SOMEBODY! YOU ARE — SOMEBODY! YOU ARE — SOMEBODY! These words of assurance have been repeatedly spoken by the Reverend Jessie Jackson, Founder of "Operation Push," and former aspirant to the high political office of the United States presidency. He encouraged thousands to register to vote, he encouraged others to turn from use of narcotics and alcohol, and encouraged all to become useful individuals in today's society by becoming one who contributes good and positive values to our society.

Jesse Jackson

A. YOUNG PEOPLE FROM PUBERTY INTO YOUNG ADULTHOOD of their twenties are seriously "SEEKING FOR THE MEANING OF LIFE." In reality, they are seeking for their niche in life. They seem bewildered by adult values, and frustrated by what seems to be hypocrisy of society. Some young people express total rejection of adult values by taking an attitude of defiance toward parental guidance, and any authority which seems to channel their actions into certain molds.

Some young people want freedom to develop and pursue a lifestyle which is totally foreign to what they deem as the "old folks" way of life. Yet, they depend upon the old folks to furnish their needs while they "do their thing" without interference from the old folks.

Still other young folks become befuddled and frustrated until they simply see no way things can improve. **To them,** educational standards are antiquated, and teachers are not qualified, nor care about the students. Thus, their poor grades are the fault of others. Love affairs **gone sour,** account for much teenage misery, fickle friends, "stab them in the back," and parents "who just don't understand" are all a constant source of insurmountable problems. These problems which seem to have no solution lead to **deep depression,** and sometimes, to thoughts of suicide.

But young folks: take courage. *Things are not as bad as they seem.* **YOU ARE LOVED, even though you may not have earned a place in society.** Yes, LOVE IS NOT EARNED, BUT IS A FREE GIFT, often lavished upon the unlovely and undeserving.

But remember: YOU ARE — SOMEBODY!!! Yes, it is up to you to **develop ideas, attitudes, and works of value if you aspire to BE SUCCESSFUL IN THIS LIFE. The future is yours, but you must "reach out" and grasp it while you are young.**

BUT PLEASE DO NOT EXPECT OTHERS TO DO FOR YOU WHAT YOU MUST DO FOR YOURSELF, FOR **YOU, TOO — CAN BE SUCCESSFUL!!!**

"Youth is not a time of life: it is a state of mind."
— *Samuel Ullman*

"There is no substitute for preparation."

B. MIDDLE AGED? YOU, TOO, CAN BE SUCCESSFUL.

Many people from young to middle age adulthood have come to regard themselves as FAILURES IN LIFE. Some people have worked at a job for years — hating to go every day, and relieved every day at quitting time. These people did not really choose their occupation. They just sort of *fell into it for lack of anything else to do,* and because the necessity to *make a living* was urgent at the time.

Perhaps, you have had a secret consuming desire to satisfy that deep longing to pursue another type of work altogether. You have felt "stuck" in an unrewarding, boring occupation because you "needed the money" for necessities of life.

Some of you have denied yourself the pleasure of pursuing your dream because it "seemed so silly" to make a living by doing that which you always considered a hobby or plaything.

Perhaps you have been *successful by the world's standard* through gaining promotions on the job, even if received purely by seniority rights. Or you have made enough money to live in a reasonably comfortable lifestyle. A lovely townhouse well appointed, with period furniture, a cabin on the lake or in the mountains, several automobiles of quality, clothes, a good bank account along with other assets have all been yours.

You have gained friends, and enjoy pomp, prestige, and popularity, yet, life seems to be void of true enjoyment. You even enjoy holding an office in the church. Still there is something missing. Friends may often become boring, the facade of pretense is taking its toll, and the old "rat race" has become a "drag" trying to keep up with the Jones'es, and all because you are living by the world's standard.

May I suggest that you stop pretending that you are happy and start looking into those ideals which you have long relegated to the background of your mind. Seek out those values you really believe in and start working toward a change which will not only be productive, but which will also make you happy!

If your family is young, working toward your goal may require some time. If your children are grown and gone, then start right away to explore your hidden desires in view of a change. Although children may grow up, they seem to always be **dependent on your financial help.** Let them pursue and finance their own goals while *you seek your own happiness for a change.*

Read on to explore and utilize the steps outlined for your guidance. **As you move on to retirement status, you may well be able to implement a new set of values** which will bring you as much joy as the birth of your firstborn child did some years ago.

"God asks no man whether he will accept life. You must take it. The only choice is how."
— *Henry Ward Beecher*

C. ARE YOU A "SENIOR CITIZEN?" YOU, TOO, CAN BE SUCCESSFUL!!!

Have you retired, or about to retire? What are your plans for the future? **Surely, you don't plan to hibernate like a bear,** nor **throw in the towel** like a defeated boxer. Please remember: YOU ARE SOMEBODY!!! YOU ARE STILL NEEDED IN YOUR SOCIETY. Yes, you can still live a productive life, helping others, **and be** happy in the process.

Perhaps your children are grown and gone, and your grandchildren are no doubt a great source of joy for you. Perhaps, you are **just plain tired and want to rest a while, and do nothing for a change.** Perhaps, your hobbies have been neglected while you gave yourself to fulfilling obligated and some voluntary services in your business, government service, firm, or other type work. But you are finished with all that now, so you can catch up on your fishing, hunting, sewing, painting, gardening, visiting, or "churchwork."

GOOD! You are following the **natural trend** of retirees who just want to get away from the "old rat race." BUT, have you realized that retirement is *not really a time to be lazy?* **We must not only keep busy, but must also remain productive for the sake of others.**

HAPPINESS IS A BY-PRODUCT OF AN EFFORT TO MAKE SOMEONE ELSE HAPPY.
— *Gretta Palmer*

Yes, **now is the time to seriously think about turning your education, experiences, talents, expertise, and compassion in a new direction.** *Now is the time to make FULL USE of the valuable wisdom which God has given you, by seeking to engage in a NEW, BUT PRODUCTIVE VENTURE WHICH WILL HELP OTHERS AS WELL AS MAKE YOU HAPPY.*

You must make the decision as to what line of service you will follow, but, consider the guidelines set forth in this book to help make the transition easier.

No doubt, the *question of age* will either enter your mind, or else be brought up by others. Please be assured my friend: AGE HAS NOTHING TO DO WITH GOOD WORKS. Some of the best works recorded in history have been accomplished by persons at or what we consider beyond retirement age.

Plato, Polycarp, John, the Apostle, Galileo, Samuel Clemens, Benjamin Franklin, Sigmund Freud, Albert Einstein, George W. Carver, Henry Ford, Winston Churchill, and Franklin D. Roosevelt, have all been persons who accomplished their greatest works in the latter days of their life. And many people exercise more **brainpower at 80 and beyond** than others of lesser age and durability.

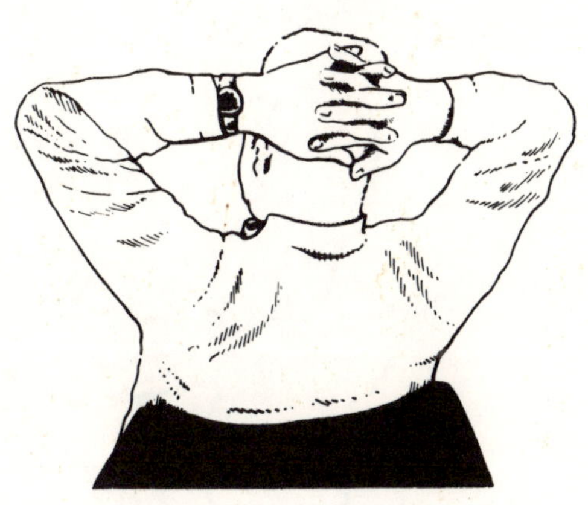

AT ANY AGE — YOU ARE SOMEBODY!!!

Even though one may not enjoy **full health** in advanced age, he or she can still contribute something to others who are not as talented as you. And speaking of **talent:**

"NO MAN POSSESSES A GENIUS SO COM-MANDING THAT HE CAN ATTAIN EMINENCE, UNLESS A SUBJECT SUITED TO HIS *TALENTS* SHOULD PRESENT ITSELF, AND AN OPPOR-TUNITY OCCUR FOR THEIR DEVELOPMENT."
— *Pliny the Elder*

So dear friend, why not utilize *your* talents in **our** needy society? After all, **being lazy in retirement soon gets boring.** So you've got to be doing *something.* RIGHT? RIGHT!!! Now, since the Lord has blessed you to live this long, why not get started on your *new venture?* **YOU ARE SOMEBODY, SO GET GOING!!!**

D. ARE YOU A PARENT?
   YOU, TOO, CAN BE SUCCESSFUL!!!

Lo, children are an heritage of the Lord: and the fruit of the womb is His reward. (to parents) *Psalm 127:3 KJV.*

Parents, you have been blessed of the Lord, because He has given you a child or children. With most material gifts, the response is a sincere "thank you" to the giver. Then the proper **use of that material gift** is further evidence of deep appreciation to the donor for the gift.

The "gift of a child to parents" is of **much more value,** for this is a human life **which is made in the spiritual image of God.** But, it is not enough to just say "thank you" to the Lord for a newborn child, for parents have the responsibility to **"Train up a child in the way he should go: and when he is old, (an adult), he will not depart from it." (right teaching)** [*Proverbs 22:6 KJV*].

Furthermore, **"Parents, do not irritate your children, but bring them up with Christian discipline and instruction."** *Ephesians 6:4 Twentieth Century New Testament.* Let us face the facts: Just as **God has given children to parents, God has also given parents to children, and, PARENTS ARE NOT AUTOMATICALLY EQUIPPED TO REAR CHILDREN.** They must learn the **SUCCESSFUL WAY TO REAR CHILDREN.** The *way we were reared is not necessarily the way all children should be reared.* **These Scriptural guidelines are the best authority we have if we would be SUCCESSFUL in being good parents.**

It is **also necessary to start our children on the road to SUCCESS** by proper upbringing in teaching values of discipline. Young people **do** have very definite ideas which they consider *crucial* in providing them with values and skills essential to SUCCESSFUL home, school, and social life. *Let us see what they say:*

PARENTS CAN DO MANY THINGS TO MOTIVATE CHILDREN TO DO THEIR BEST.

PARENTS CAN:

1. **SET EXAMPLES** through their own conduct, and explain to us the values underlying **why they do things a certain way.**

2. **SHARE PERSONAL PAST EXPERIENCE** and family stories which reinforces the message that sincere effort, persistence, and good character count.

3. **GIVE US RESPONSIBILITIES** at home to foster self-worth, resourcefulness, and to help to establish work routines.

4. **TEACH US TO PLAN AHEAD** by requiring that we complete schoolwork and household chores **before** indulging in recreation.

5. **PRAISE OUR GOOD BEHAVIOR AND PERFORMANCE** as well as correct our misconduct. As children, it is important to us to know **what behavior** you find acceptable. And as I am being corrected, help me to know that **you still love me.**

6. ENCOURAGE EACH OF US TO COMPETE and give **our best effort** to SUCCEED in our studies in the same way we might compete in sports. Parents should realize that children are sometimes **pressured by peers to not do well in academics.** So, understanding, support, and encouragement are needed to help us to resist such pressure.

7. ESTABLISH FAMILY RULES by setting a curfew time to be home, a bedtime hour, and limits on outside activities.

8. EXPECT TO REVIEW HOMEWORK ASSIGN-MENTS on a regular basis, and provide a quiet well-equipped place for study time.

9. MAKE EFFECTIVE USE OF HOME LEISURE TIME. This could include talking about school experiences, selecting proper friendships, being selective about **T.V. program choices** and viewing times, and simply communicating **without yelling.**

10. SHOW SUPPORT FOR THE SCHOOL AND TEACHERS by getting us off on time with needed schoolwork and supplies.

11. VISIT THE SCHOOL SOME TIMES, and help other parents to improve our school. Volunteer to help the school staff when possible.

12. TEACH US AT HOME TO REVERENCE AND WORSHIP GOD by saying "table grace," learning Bible verses and **let us children hear you pray sometimes that we might also learn to pray openly and in sincerity.**

SUCCESSFUL PARENTS HELP STIMULATE CHIL-DREN TO BECOME **SUCCESSFUL.**

SET A GOOD EXAMPLE FOR YOUR CHILDREN. CHILDREN *DO* LEARN BY EXAMPLE!

— Notes —

CHAPTER II.

PREPARING TO BE SUCCESSFUL.

THERE IS NO SUBSTITUTE FOR PREPARATION! This statement is repeated because of its importance to becoming really successful. Success does not seek the individual, but the individual must seek for that which he aspires to become. I believe the seeking must start from within the individual and work out through the seeker.

Do not by any means depend upon **luck,** if indeed it happens to exist. Personally, I do not believe in luck — good, nor bad. However, **if you believe in luck,** many will warn you that Lady Luck can be as elusive as a slippery eel.

In your pursuits to gain that which you seek, many friends will admire your spunk, pat you on the back, and wish you the best. Some especially close friends might even assure you that should their help be needed, they will surely be there for you. What great encouragement this statement gives to the seeker, but *don't depend on it!* Friends are always making good-sounding promises, and most of them truly mean what they say, **but,** at the very time you need them the most, they are either out of town, indisposed, or tied up with personal problems. Even when they are available you may be delayed for a time longer than you desire t wait.

So, I suggest that you not depend on anybody, no, not even on members of your household. Yes, they love you and share your ambitions to a point, but they are also busy doing their own thing. Furthermore, **many doors of opportunity are not opened by human ingenuity**. Therefore, let us establish this fact now: I **personally believe that God directs my steps, opens doors of opportunity before me, and closes doors of adversity behind me.** And what He does for me, He will do for you. In fact, the Lord *might do more for you as you yield yourself more fully for His guidance.*

Now, do not expect the Lord nor any humans, whether friend or family members to do for you the things you should do for yourself. For the fact remains: There is no substitute for preparation, the preparation which **you must make before reaping rewards.** IF YOU ARE **NOT READY** FOR THIS PART OF THE WORK, THEN READ NO FURTHER.

Now friend, if you are still with me, let us proceed to involve ourselves in the preparation which seems so important to your mission.

A. DESIRE TO BE SUCCESSFUL.

In his "Essays on Humanity," Victor Hugo says: **"The deep essence of life, it is in thee that it must be looked for. Geniuses are begotten from thee, mysterious crowd."**

Yes, the desire to succeed must lie within the individual. The greater the desire, the more diligent the search to fulfill that desire. To be desirous means to have a longing, yearning, eager aspiration to obtain something of value. In our study, **we are not speaking of obtaining tangible goods** just for the sake of possession. But **we speak primarily of attainment of an intangible, value of personal worth** in our society.

Certainly, to be considered a worthwhile person, one must be able to stand on merit, somewhat independent of obligations to others, yet, providing something of value to others.

So, please examine yourself to determine if you have that deep-seated desire born of aspiration to succeed. Now, go on to the next step.

B. OBSERVE OTHERS WHO ARE SUCCESSFUL.

Since your desire for attainment is sufficiently motivated, you need to **observe others already working in the field in which you are interested.** You will find many who have attained various degrees of notoriety, whether or not they are successful. The examples you see will be of much value to you since it is said: "One picture is worth a thousand words." Although you may see many examples, all of them will not appeal to you. So *select only those examples where success is obvious* and forget the poor or mediocre.

I am not suggesting that you should be covetous in desire, for to covet means to have an inordinate desire for wealth of possessions that belong to another. A second definition of covetousness means to entertain a greedy avaricious attitude of selfishness.

I am suggesting however, that you should select the **best examples available of those serving in your field** of interest. Everyone needs a *role model,* but only those worthy of emulation should be considered. A role model need not be perfect, so do not become *too critical* of others. But do not waste time on anything or anyone that does not thrill you or capture your imagination.

Seeking direction from the Lord will bring to your attention the most creditable and genuine prospects for your purpose. So do not be reluctant to ask the Almighty for divine guidance. After all, you are seeking the best, and He alone knows who are the best.

C. SUCCESS RELATES TO HAPPINESS

Excerpts from a book called "Happy People," written and copyrighted by Jonathan L. Freedman in 1978 gives results from research he had done in the field of psychology.

His research reveals much that is new and reassuring about happiness. For example:

☆ People **do not become less happy** as they grow older.
☆ Money **can't buy** happiness.
☆ Unhappy **children are not doomed** to be unhappy adults.
☆ **Most Americans** are happy.

Other surveys of his overall findings seem to be representative of the nation in general. Here are some patterns that emerged:

a) **Love and Sex:**

Those who love and are loved in return are happier than others. You can be happy **without** a good sex life, and you can **have** a good sex life and **still be unhappy.**

b) **Marriage:**

A vast majority of our population seem to find happiness in marriage, and **become unhappy** if they **remain single too long.**

c) **The Single Life:**

Single men and women are generally less happy than married ones. After age 40 the "happiness gap" between single and married men seems to disappear. However, for many reasons, life seems particularly **hard for single women as they age.**

d) **Divorce:**

Those who are **divorced are much less happy,** so it comes as no surprise that most divorced people eventually remarry. **For men,** the second marriage is happier than the first. But, women, on the average, seem slightly less happy in a second marriage.

e) **Working Wives:**

One question in the survey asked people if they suffered from headache, sleeplessness, worries, loneliness, etc. Professor Freedman found: **Married women who do not work** are much more likely to have these kinds of symptoms. **Employed wives** are less anxious and worried, and less likely to be unhappy than housewives.

WORKING WIVES ARE HAPPIER

f) **Age and Happiness:**
Despite widespread belief that the middle years are the happiest, the survey shows this is not so. **Neither does getting old mean that one will become more unhappy.**

Major factors contributing to unhappiness **in older age** are reduced income, loss of a spouse, and the boredom of retirement. In fact, older people are **more likely** to say that they are very happy, than any other age group in the survey.

g) **Income and Education:**
The influence of money and education on happiness seems to depend on one's original expectations for his life. Those who expected to earn much because of their extensive education, find little happiness in success. The happiest groups were those with little education who earned a lot; while the highly educated who earned a lot were not so well off psychologically.

h) **Job and Happiness:**
Satisfaction with your work is a more important element of happiness than anything, **except love and marriage.** Happiness of workers revealed that clerks were at the bottom of the range. Ranging upward in happiness were: secretaries, blue-collar workers, architects, college professors, nurses and managers. **At the top** of the contentment scale came clergy-men, psychologists, and entertainers.

JOB SATISFACTION MAKES ONE HAPPY

Professor Freedman indicated that lawyers and doctors rated themselves as relatively unhappy.

i) **Childhood and Adolescence:**
Teen-age happiness is no measurement of a successfully happy life which one can experience as an adult. This is true because **as one matures, values usually change drastically.**

Is there such a thing as a **"recipe for happiness"?** Recurring elements in the lives of people considered **very happy** suggests these answers:

1. To love and be loved in return.

2. To have enough money, but not necessarily a great deal.

3. To have meaning and direction in life.

4. To have a sense of control over your own life.

5. To have received more from life than you expected.

THE SHREWD MAN OF BUSINESS WILL SUCCEED WELL, BUT THE HAPPY MAN IS HE WHO TRUSTS IN THE LORD.
Proverbs 16:20 [New English Bible]

OBSERVE OTHERS WHO ARE SUCCESSFUL

— Notes —

CHAPTER III.

WORK TO BECOME SUCCESSFUL.

Work can be considered involvement in a job, occupation, calling, task, craftsmanship, toil, or function which produces an end results for efforts.

PRODUCER

For practical purposes, people may be categorized into two groups: Group 1. are termed **producers.** These are people who regularly and routinely work at producing merchandise or services of value. Those in this category may produce from meagerly to abundantly, yet, they **always produce more than they consume.** Consequently, these producers always leave their job, or society, or the world better off than they found it.

Group 2. are termed **users.** These are people who will not work regularly, if at all. They seldom produce anything of value, but, if they produce, they always manage to **use up all they produce, plus**

USER

what others produce. People in this category are considered leaches or parasites on society. They create a strain on family and government by draining off values which could be reinvested for the *common good.* USERS ARE NEVER SUCCESSFUL BECAUSE THEY PUT FORTH NO EFFORT TO PROSPER BY THEIR OWN WORK.

In all probability, older adults and senior citizens have contributed much to the workforce, laboring diligently down through the years. Their contributions to family, society, and government speaks for itself. Those few who have not made substantial contributions may be those chronically ill or the handicapped. Certainly, this is not their fault.

The greater possibility of non-producers may be adolescents from thirteen through twenty-one years old. Those in this age bracket have not been trained or developed to the point of service because they are still in their formative years. **If you are in this age group, please learn to work at a legal profitable occupation.**

It is assumed that adults twenty-two and upward have been schooled or trained to work, serve, and lead in productive occupations. Your youth, strength, and ingenuity are great assets which helps to build our country.

If you are a young adult with no training or special skills for. the workforce, you *still have time* and hopefully, opportunity to realize your desires and goals. Sometimes, trade schools or vocational schools can provide a trade background at reasonable cost. Please look into these possibilities!

Regardless to age bracket, or station in life, *all people should seek to engage in an occupation suitable to their taste.* In the forefront of accomplishment is always WORK! WORK! WORK! And work must be accompanied by purpose, and with purpose.

HE WHO WOULD ARRIVE AT THE APPOINTED END MUST FOLLOW A SINGLE ROAD, AND NOT WANDER THROUGH MANY WAYS.
—Seneca

Mr. Eugene Kendall, in his letter to "Your Views" of the Daily Oklahoman in Oklahoma City has some valuable suggestions for youth of today. His letter states:

American students have had the attitude that "I don't have to work or study hard. I can have a good time in high school and college and get a good job without knowing math, science, and all that junk."

But this is no longer true. Because of drugs, alcohol, and this bad attitude in American schools, America is about to produce an uneducated, undisciplined generation and will be a second-class country in the 21st century if all American students do not understand and believe these facts of life and change their attitude 180 degrees:

1. If you drop out you can never have a good job and will have a very difficult future unless you drop back in.

2. If you use or sell drugs, you will have no future... none. In a short time you will either be in jail for a long term, executed for murder, be murdered by gang members, or have AIDS.

3. If you do not use drugs, stay in school, learn all you can and graduate from high school, you can with on-the-job-training, improve yourself and your job, have a good future and a good life.

4. If you graduate from high school and take extra Vo-tech, junior college or other training, you can get a much better job and have a much better future.

5. If you graduate from college you can have your choice of many excellent jobs at an excellent salary. You can have a nice family, home, and a pleasant life. You can do even better with a post-graduate or professional degree.

You **future is entirely up to you!** You must decide what you want your life to be. The government and the business world do realize that unless students stay off of drugs, stay in school and get the best education they can, America will become a second-class country very soon, so they are going to see that no student is educationally limited for lack of finances. **If you understand and believe this, your future can be GREAT,** and you can become **SUCCESSFUL!!!**

DON'T BE A DROPOUT!

A. RESEARCH YOUR SUBJECT FOR SUCCESS.

"Ask, and it shall be given you; SEEK AND YE SHALL FIND; knock, and it shall be opened unto you."
— *Matthew 7:7*

Fortunately, books have been written on just about *everything.* So, there probably is a book written on the subject in which you are interested, whether the subject is on science, arts, humanities, hobbies, athletics, or what have you. Books are mostly available at libraries for loan, or in bookstores for sale. One should also watch for newspaper articles, and magazines published on the subject in which you are interested.

Another arm of research involves **learning by interviews.** Most people love to talk about their field of endeavor, so find these people. If you are impressed by their accomplishments, or you want to learn their system or style of operation, then *talk to them and ask questions.* Do not trust your memory, write down what they tell you, then sort out the information later.

Still, another arm of research to consider involves the fact of specific location where your role model's work is carried out. For instance, if you are interested in learning the art of pottery making, you would do well to go to the site where this work is being performed. Remember, **"one picture is worth a thousand words."** It is possible that you might get to tour the place at little or no expense, and the knowledge gained should certainly offset the cost of going to the location. Again, **write down what you see.** This includes each step taken in the process from beginning to end.

If your mind is "still fuzzy" concerning the project, it may be wise to review the professionally written books to clarify what was not previously understood. After all, *your primary purpose for research at this point* is to determine whether or not you want to pursue a certain occupation for profit, or a certain hobby for fun or self-fulfillment. You may also decide to go to something else altogether. Anyway, the end result of your research will help you determine if you should invest any time, effort, and money into this venture.

Also, remember, your main goal is to BECOME SUCCESSFUL IN A VENTURE OF YOUR CHOOSING, AND BEING HAPPY IN THE PROCESS. **If you are not sure by now** that you are making the right choice, then your "inner feelings" are saying **NO** to this particular job. *Go back and start looking for something else* that you can be comfortable with.

If your research has made you **more enthusiastic about your choice, then,** *let us go to the next work step in the process of becoming successful.*

RESEARCH YOUR SUBJECT FOR SUCCESS

B.   LEARN YOUR SUBJECT FOR SUCCESS.

In the social world of people, "familiarity breeds contempt." In the world of industry, familiarity leads to success. Researching your subject has led you to embrace the psychological aspects of your new venture. Your thoughts are racing from point to point. Your enthusiasm is increasing even as you read this guideline. THAT'S GOOD!!!

Now, your next task is to learn about the subject which has made you so enthusiastic. By this I mean, **theory must be transformed into reality.** This step requires that one learn the mechanics of the new venture.

1. **IF YOU ARE A YOUNG ADULT AND NEW IN THE JOB MARKET,** then hopefully your educational background will be valuable in assisting you to start your own business, or to locate with an existing company or firm where you can put your education to use.

If you are *not* **educated nor have any special skills** in your field of interest, try to locate a Vo-tech of trade school which offers courses of training which will benefit you.

Some companies may have (or should have) an AP-PRENTICE PROGRAM where uneducated or unskilled persons may learn by **on-the-job training.** The pay may be Minimum Wage rates or slightly above, but that beats nothing. *Please do not tell others nor delude yourself into thinking, "I can do anything." The fact is: Without education or skills, you can do nothing.* There is **no market for those skilled in doing nothing.**

2. **IF YOU ARE ALREADY IN THE JOB MARKET AND SEEKING A MORE SATISFYING OCCUPATION,** there are a few things you might consider.

If your desire is to **go to an entirely new occupation,** and you have sufficient finances to sustain you indefinitely, then set a time frame to *make a complete break* with your present situation. Then, go full steam at the new venture.

If you cannot go that strong, then you may be able to devote spare time to the new venture while remaining in your present occupation. Overtime effort will be required, and it will take much longer to attain your goal, but working at your leisure will be quite satisfying.

If you are near retirement age or position, you may set the stage to begin the new venture at the time you elect to retire from the present job. As an example: Suppose you are interested in canvas painting. You have time to seek out and purchase the proper canvas, painting, easels, paints, brushes, and related supplies. You also have time to study art forms, set up a present room or add on a special room as a studio, and even "dabble" around before leaving the present job.

3. IF YOU ARE A SENIOR CITIZEN RETIRED FROM THE JOB MARKET, you may be just "itching" to get started on your new venture. With your maturity, your research has helped you make a definite decision to get involved with a lifelong ambition long relegated to the background.

If you are affluent or derive income from several sources, then retirement does not mean paucity of income. So there is no problem with living expense or investing in a venture which interests you. **You have the time to invest** since you are already retired with **no one to "boss" you. You have the money to invest** since you are not a pauper in dire need of every penny you own. **You have wisdom and skills to invest,** since no one can live to retire and not learn *something.* **You have good will to invest,** since you have read to this point. So, **get started in enjoying the rest of your life.**

If you are retired with a moderate income, you still deserve to have a SUCCESSFUL LIFE. Your choice of a new venture may mean **utilizing what you have.** Such

GARDENING

things as gardening in the back yard, repairing or refinishing furniture in your garage, making quilts, doilies, or dolls in that extra bedroom, can add to your pleasure of life.

THE REWARD OF A THING WELL DONE, IS TO HAVE DONE IT.
— *Emerson*

Perhaps you are retired with a modest income or even on welfare, *do not despair. You, too, can be successful!* People who have little, are best qualified to sympathize with others who have nothing. You may have little or no finances to contribute to others in need, yet I **firmly believe that God gives everyone something by which he may help others.** Even without wealth there are values we can contribute to the lives of others which benefit them, and make us happy in the process.

Volunteer service to hospitals, visitation to shut-ins at convalescent homes are much in demand.   Some governmental programs hire low income people to provide a few hours of basic care each day to the indigent citizens, and some senior citizens hire out to "fast food chains," and get much joy along with a few dollars in the process.

I personally know a man who retired from an upper eschelon government job several years ago. With retirement, Social Security, and several profitable investments, he was not in financial need. Yet, one day I found him sacking groceries at a local chainstore. Working energetically, and smiling

INDOOR GARDENING

gleefully, he explained: I have **always wanted to work in a grocery store, and now that I have my chance, I'm as happy as can be."**

THERE IS AN HOUR WHEREIN A MAN MIGHT BE HAPPY ALL HIS LIFE, COULD HE FIND IT.
— *George Herbert*

C. SEVEN STEPS THAT LEAD TO PEAK PERFORMANCE.

An article by Morton Hunt that appeared in Reader's Digest in September 1982, gives good insight on becoming a high achiever. He cites work done by the Peak Performance Center, in Berkeley, California, which was headed by Charles Garfield.

Mr. Garfield's Research Institute had studied 1500 outstanding achievers in nearly every walk of life and found that they all have certain traits in common, not necessarily inborn, but which can be learned by anyone.

This does not mean that **everyone** will automatically get to the top of their chosen field. But, it does mean that all of us can learn to utilize our talents to the maximum. So, based on Garfield's research, here are **several steps that can lead to peak performance.**

1. Lead a well-rounded life.
We have heard that high achievers are usually "Type A" personalities who are hard-driving, obsessed people, who often bring work home, and they often labor until bedtime. However, these people tend to peak early, decline, and level off. They become addicted to work itself, with little concern for results.

In contrast, **high performers** do work hard, but within strict limits. They know how to relax sometimes, leave work at the office, and spend moderate time with their family and friends.

2. Select a career you care about.
Garfield's data show that **high performers** choose work they truly prefer, and spend over two-thirds of their working hours doing it and only one-third on chores they dislike.

These are the people that want **internal** satisfaction, not just **external** rewards such as raises, promotions, and power. Of course, in the end, they usually have both. **Why?** Because they enjoy what they are doing, their work is better and their rewards higher.

3. Rehearse each task mentally.
Before any important or difficult situation is fully determined, **most peak performers** run through the desired actions in their minds over and over again. This

deliberate mental workout hones and fine tunes the skills actually needed in the accomplishment of their intended task. It is said: a pianist imprisoned in China for seven years during the Cultural Revolution, played as well as ever soon after he was released. His explanation: *"I practiced everyday in my mind."*

REHEARSE EACH TASK MENTALLY

4. Seek results, not perfection.
Many ambitious, hard-working people become so **obsessed with perfection** in their work that they get very little work done. They become so involved in minor details that their overall accomplishments suffer.

High performers are mostly free of compulsion to be perfect. They don't usually think of their mistakes as failures. Instead, they learn from those mistakes so they may do better next time.

5. Be willing to take a risk.
Most people prefer to stay in the "comfort zone" of their work. This means, they **settle for security,** even if it means boredom and producing a mediocre work.

High performers, by contrast, are willing to take risks because they carefully consider how they would adjust to salvage the situation — if in fact they did fail. This means making an allowance for failure without being paralyzed by fear of failure. One who is immobilized by fear has no chance at all.

6. Do not underestimate your potential.
Most of us think we know our own limits. But much of what we "know" isn't knowledge at all but belief — **self limiting beliefs.** "And self-limiting beliefs," says Garfield, "are the biggest obstacle to high level performance."

High performers, on the other hand, are better able to ignore artificial barriers. They concentrate on themselves — on their feelings, on their functioning, and on the momentum of their efforts. They are therefore better able to achieve at peak levels.

7. Compete with yourself, not with others.
High performers focus more intently on **making their own previous efforts better** than on beating someone else's efforts. Since most high performers are interested in doing a better job **by their own standards,** they are not always loners, but tend to be "team players."

They recognize that others can help solve certain problems better than individuals. So they are willing to get help from others to do the work which they cannot do themselves.

Such are the **skills of high performers.** Lastly, Mr. Garfield further explains: "I am not saying try harder, or why don't you do better?" I **am** saying, you have the power to change your habits of mind and acquire certain skills. If you choose to do so, you can improve your performance, your productivity, and the **quality of your whole life.**

DON'T BE AFRAID — VENTURE OUT!

SUMMARY OF CHAPTERS I, II, and III.

In order to reinforce what we have talked about in the past three chapters, we should observe that three things have been required:

1. COMMITMENT TO THE IDEA OF BEING SUCCESSFUL.

2. SUBMITTING TO PREPARATION TO BECOME SUCCESSFUL.

3. WORKING AT THE TASK OF BECOMING SUCCESSFUL.

COMMITMENT:

Just as one is not born full grown, neither does success come full blown. There must first be a desire born of inspiration. One is never "too young," or "too old" to have aspirations to achieve his idea of success. **Therefore, one may succeed beyond his fondest dreams, but, will never succeed without a dream.** Even so, a dream or desire must be followed by commitment in order to become reality.

SUBMITTING:

One who is willing to prepare before jumping headlong into his new venture has the greatest chance to succeed. This means "learning the ropes" through research, observation, and interviewing others who already fit our ideal or a successful person. Although not previously mentioned, I believe it is also important to turn aside from other interests which contribute nothing to our number one priority. Once your decision is made, time becomes of the essence in moving toward fulfillment. Also, remember, **there is no substitute for preparation.**

WORKING:

To work is to **put into practice that which we have dreamed of, prepared for, and ultimately hope to attain.** This means active involvement in the mechanics of the venture. No one can guarantee complete accomplishment without a few times of opposition or reversals. Nevertheless, these can be overcome with the proper ATTITUDES on our part, which we shall discuss next. Let us also realize that **half the fun of accomplishment is derived from applying ourselves to the task.** Victory without battle is like a bucket with a hole in it; the valuable contents are missing.

THE TALENT OF SUCCESS IS NOTHING MORE THAN DOING WHAT YOU CAN DO WELL, AND DOING WELL, WHATEVER YOU DO.   — *Longfellow*

WORK TO BECOME SUCCESSFUL!!!

— Notes —

CHAPTER IV.

ATTITUDES CAN MAKE YOU SUCCESSFUL!!!

If you are still reading this guideline for becoming successful, you will surely realize that we have exhausted human effort to gain success. Now the **non-mechanical** attributes of becoming successful must be considered and discussed for true fulfillment of our dream for **REAL SUCCESS.**

Perhaps there are many who cannot equate worldly attainments with spiritual values. This is especially true of those whose main goal is the attainment of monetary or other worldly values. They want no spiritual restraints or religious hindrances which might impede their pursuit of wealth or other goals which may be **less than honorable.** Indeed, ambition born of selfishness seeks to circumvent any restrictive ideas which may cause the conscience to rebel.

However, as a Christian, I am convinced that ATTITUDES play a very important role in ones life, whether or not he is a Christian. So, *if you are still with me,* let us consider the **attitudes of FAITH, HOPE, AND LOVE,** in our quest for a true fulfillment of **successful living.**

In all honesty, I have come to realize that **true success is not measured in terms of worldly gain or wealth, but, in terms of contentment.** This is especially true for middle-aged or senior citizens who have already earned their money. But for young people just getting started in life, wealth, position, and other industrial advantages seem to be their measure of successfulness. Yet, **young people, you can have a reasonable portion of this world's goods, and still not cheat society** if you are willing to adopt the spiritual attitudes that measure the real man.

JUST HOW DOES FAITH, HOPE, AND LOVE MAKE A DIFFERENCE in our pursuits?

1. Man is limited in human ability to accomplish what he desires because of limited knowledge and understanding.

2. Man cannot discern the future, so his choices may be unwise and contrary to God's Will for his life.

3. Man is easily discouraged when reversals come, unless spiritual forces from within sustain him.

4. Man must be at peace with society if he will "make his mark" in society, since "no man is an isle" unto himself.

5. Man is nothing without God, so **true, lasting, real success cannot be attained nor sustained without the Lord.**

So it seems that ones' **commitment, submission, and work** must extend beyond human efforts into the spiritual realm of faith, hope, and love. BELIEVE ME, WITHOUT THESE VIRTUES, ANY SUCCESS YOU MAY ACHIEVE WILL NOT BRING HAPPINESS!!!

A. EXERCISING FAITH TO BECOME SUCCESSFUL

Now faith is a confident assurance of that for which we hope, a conviction of the reality of things we do not see. — The New Testament in Modern Speech [*Richard Weymouth*].

When seeking that which is of **vital interest** to life, one **should never** rely solely upon human intellect, understanding, nor ingenuity. As we assimilated the information previously suggested, it is hoped that we are in harmony with the steps set forth. Implementation of these steps is meant to set the human ingenuity to work, for without human effort, there is no need to seek spiritual attainment of our goals. But the fact is, *with human effort alone,* we soon come to the stone wall of doubt and despair.

At this point, we become desperately in need of a spiritual value outside of self **which we can rely upon** to propel us past this wall of doubt. Thus, the human ingenuity is reinforced by the more powerful and dependable spiritual virtue of faith.

The definition of faith given above emphasizes the positive aspect of a "confident assurance" of that for which we are seeking. Up to this point, human effort could give us no real guarantee of being successful in our venture, but FAITH *with human effort assures the seeker,* for faith convinces us that the *reality* of our goal is indeed available.

In conversing with many people engaged in various fields of endeavor, more than half of them express **much faith in themselves to accomplish.** However, **I am not among those who have achieved anything of value through faith in SELF.** But I *can* say truthfully that a

small degree of confidence in human effort on my part *plus* **a great degree of FAITH IN MY GOD has wrought miracles in my life.** Just what is so important about the spiritual value of faith in ones' seeking?

Well, I can explain better if you will permit me to use the term *Christian faith* rather than the term *spiritual faith.* Christian faith expresses *belief* in a personal living God that is aware of not only needs, but also the aspirations of His people. And because He is concerned for us, we can easily acknowledge the fact of His supremeness, and ability to acomplish for us that which we cannot accomplish for ourselves. So, in reality, the **COMMITMENT TO THE IDEA OF BEING SUCCESSFUL** previously discussed is not an abstract notion, but a concrete commitment to our Father who alone can turn an idea into a true and living fact.

SUBMITTING TO PREPARATION TO BECOME SUC-CESSFUL is not a submission to self nor to a work schedule which seems to be a necessary step to gain success. To me, the submission must be to the Lord who is able to give guidance and direction to the individual. **Thus our submission to God gives Him the opportunity to infuse into our uncertain ideas a measure of certainty which will not backfire later.**

WORKING AT THE TASK OF BECOMING SUCCESSFUL

"My brothers, what is the use of anyone declaring that he has faith, if he has no deeds to show? —
— *Moffatt*

Can such faith without deeds provide his needs?
— *Smith*

"In just the same way faith, if not followed by actions is, by itself, a lifeless thing." — Twentieth Century New Testament [*James 2: 14, 17*].

Our previous discussion on **COMMITMENT TO THE IDEA, AND SUBMITTING TO PREPARATION TO BECOME SUCCESSFUL** must now be reinforced by **WORKING AT THE TASK OF BECOMING SUCCESSFUL.** The above Scriptural references are given to assure the dreamer his success is possible only as he is willing to undergird his faith by works if he would gain his dream.

We are reminded that faith is not alone, but has a twin companion that *always* parallels and fulfills the concept of accomplishment. As faith must be founded in the Deity, so must works be directed by the Deity. **Works must not be a blind venture, nor an exercise in futility, but must be seen as a positive step toward attaining the goal sought.**

I have personally wasted much time by driving to several places for interviews, information, and other assistance. Some of those trips produced *some* measure of results, but *most* of those trips were unproductive because telephone communications to set up appointments were neglected. The idea that your presence may be more commanding, does not consider the possibility that the one whose help you seek may have prior plans. Your benefactor may have another client, be on vacation, ill, or may not even be the person who can help you. Thus, valuable time has been wasted by not following proper procedure.

Also, unplanned procedure may lead not only to time waste, but also to unnecessary monetary cost. Work must be organized in order to be profitable. What the Christian lacks in proper planning may indicate a need to rely upon trust in the divine rather than human resources. That **trust** should be expressed **in prayer** for **prayer changes things** for the better, and seems to bring it all together. Through divine direction, work ceases to be a haphazard operation, eliminates many costly mistakes, and propels us toward quicker and greater accomplishment of our goal.

So, the spiritual ATTITUDE of **faith includes trusting in, and praying to our God who can bring the IDEA, PREPARATION, AND WORK ALL TOGETHER** with greater assurance, and fewer mistakes. THIS IS INDEED EXERCISING FAITH TO BECOME SUCCESS-FUL.

THE TASK OF BECOMING SUCCESSFUL!

DOES SUCCESS COME BY CHOICE OR CHANCE?

B. EXERCISING HOPE TO BECOME SUCCESSFUL

The second ATTITUDE we must exercise to become successful is HOPE. "For our salvation lies in hope:"
— *Conybeare*

"Hope always means waiting for something that we do not yet possess."
— *Phillips*

"For why should a man hope for that which he has seen?" ... "And if we are hoping for something still unseen, then we need endurance to wait for it."   — *Knox*
[Romans 8: 24-25]

These important statements emphasize the attitude of hope which is also vital to becoming successful. This Scripture specifically refers to *anticipation of salvation of soul and body* to its completion. However, hope can be applied also to other circumstances which are important to our welfare.

We must realize that many values which we hold dear are far beyond human reach or attainment. And because of our limitations we would surely despair of these values were it not for hope and its attendant attitudes.

Those of us commonly called "work-a-holics" and further designated psychologically as "type A" personalities, are highly prone to be **impatient. We usually like to have a clear field to move at will without hindrances from any source.** We like to **soar as eagles** with full pursuit towards our goal without the impedance of roadblocks. When something tends to slow us down, we work around these hindrances. But let's face it, we **are sometimes slowed to a snail's pace, and on rare occasions we are brought to a dead halt.** *The irritation becomes almost unbearable,* so we fret and fume until we can get started full steam again.

At this point, the virtue of hope becomes indispensable because **hope fosters patience.** By learning to become patient, we also experience the need for endurance, or the ability to outlast the irritation we feel when impeded. Our hope is activated by submission to God, and endurance is the result of that submission. With endurance we learn to develop a tolerance to situations that we cannot regulate. God, then not only regulates the situations, but also regulates our disposition toward these situations.

Another good virtue that springs from hope is **persistence.** This persistence is not a hostile bully-your-way-through, attitude, but helps us to actively wait until God clears the obstacles from our path. At the same time, we are working on other things to tie up loose ends. Persistence pays off as we resume our seeking of the original plan.

HOPE IS LIKE THE SUN, WHICH AS
WE JOURNEY TOWARDS IT, CASTS THE
SHADOW OF OUR BURDENS BEHIND US.
— *Samuel Smiles*

C. EXERCISING LOVE TO BECOME SUCCESSFUL

The third attitude we must exercise to become successful is LOVE.

"Do not love the world or what the world can offer. When anyone loves the world, there is no love for the Father in him." --Twentieth Century New Testament
[*I John 2: 15*]

"All that the world can offer, the things our physical nature and eyes crave for, and the proud display of life do not belong to the Father, but to the world."

— Moffatt [*I John 2:16*]

"The world and all its passionate desires will pass away, but, he who persists in doing things God's Way lives on forever." — Smith [*I John 2:17*]

My friends, you may or may not be of the Christian persuasion, and it is not my goal to change your religious beliefs. My primary intent is to assure that **YOU, TOO, CAN BE SUCCESSFUL!** It is very likely that those in mature years are highly aware that the ATTITUDES presented here are a necessary part of the *formula for true success.* It is also likely that your previous accomplishments in life were partly or completely due to spiritual values which you embrace. If so, **GOOD!!!**

To you, young readers, most of this part is designed to help you to understand the *importance* of Christian values in gaining your goal.

1. LOVE DEFINED:

The term "love" seems to be a catch-all phrase that expresses approval and like-a-bility of ideas, places, and things. It is common to hear: "I love my dress, I love my car, I love my house, I love my dog, I love certain T.V. programs, etc." Love used in this way expresses attachment for inanimate things. But love defined is a strong complex emotion of feeling which is directed toward animate objects, and specifically people. Love causes one to appreciate, delight in, and crave the presence of another. Love's desire is to please or to promote the welfare of another individual.

2. THE OBJECT OF LOVE IDENTIFIED:

The Greek language is very expressive and gives light on four different types of love. Let us consider them:

a.) EROS is a type of love expressed as affectionate feelings between husband and wife, or lover and sweetheart. This type love is fulfilled in sexual desire and completion.

b.) PHILEO is the type of love expressive of brotherly or sisterly affection as between friends.

c.) STORGE is the type of love expressive of respect and affection between members of the same family.

d.) AGAPAO is the type of love which expresses the attitude of God towards His Son, towards the human race, and towards those who believe on the Lord Jesus Christ.

3. THE OBJECT OF LOVE EXPLAINED:

Everybody loves something or somebody! One may love abstract ideas, philosophy, psychology, or other incomplete sciences. Others may love inanimate things such as possessions, art, sculpture, or buildings. Still others may love animate objects such as pets. Yet, there is a higher type of love worthy of consideration and explanation.

The AGAPAO love previously identified is the highest type love which originated with God and is expressed by God for His Creation. Since *you and I are the crowning achievement of God's creation,* He is primarily concerned about our welfare. Therefore, God's Love for us encompasses all of life in this world and the world to come. Thus, *it is God's Will that we live SUCCESSFULLY IN THIS LIFE, AND IN THE LIFE TO COME.*

The love in the **heart of God** is beyond our capability, since we are not Divine, but human. Therefore, **our love is a reflection of God's love** which is capable of response to Him in gratitude. And love can be known only by the action it prompts. Since God is concerned for others, we too must be also concerned for others. Love begins with respect and is essential for working with others.

The Scriptural references given at the beginning of this **third attitude** suggest that we not love only that which the world can offer, since those values that appeal to the physical nature will soon fail. But we are advised to direct our love **from the world and towards the Heavenly Father.** For those who persist in doing things the Lord's way will surely succeed.

Now may I again remind us, THE SUCCESS WE SEEK IS TO BE HAPPY, FULFILLING, AND PERMANENT. We are not able to fulfill this seeking because of our limitations, but the God that loves us, sustains us, and fully understands us can fulfill our seeking. With this knowledge, you can't miss. For **YOU ARE SOMEBODY, AND, YOU, TOO, CAN BE SUCCESSFUL!!!** regardless to your age or station in life.

BEING HAPPY WITH WHO YOU ARE, AND WHAT YOU ARE.

— Notes —

CHAPTER V.

PRAYING THAT YOU WILL BECOME SUCCESSFUL.

Not only is God capable but is also willing to fulfill our desires if we *seek Him through prayer.* "More things have been wrought by prayer than this world has ever known." Now if we make God the object of our love and continue in His love, then we may ask what we will [*desire*] and He will grant our requests. Remember: "Ask, and you shall receive; Seek, and you shall find; Knock, and it shall be open to you."

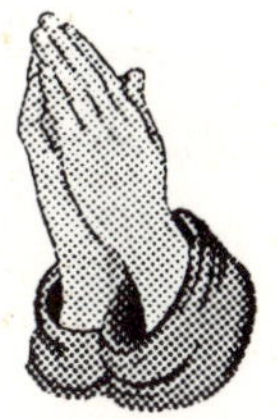

TO PRAY WELL IS THE BETTER HALF OF STUDY.
          — *Luther*
TIME SPENT ON THE KNEES IN PRAYER WILL DO MORE TO REMEDY HEART STRAIN AND NERVE WORRY THAN ANYTHING ELSE.   —*George David Steward*

MEN OUGHT ALWAYS PRAY AND NEVER GIVE UP.
          — *Luke 18:1*

The multiplied **Scriptural references to prayer, the many philosophical originations concerning prayer** by the Bards, and the untold **millions of people the world over who have EXPERIENCED the value of prayer in their own lives** is a concrete testimony that **prayer is the most persuasive power known to man.**

There is no disgrace brought upon one who submits to prayer. For to pray or to submit the self to prayer is an acknowledgement of incompleteness on the part of the seeker. Therefore, the seeker desires fulfillment and completeness.

A. PRAYER FROM THE HUMAN POINT OF VIEW:

What Some People Think:

1. **Some people think that prayer is an admission of weakness** with inability to "pull off" a deal that was "shaky" from the beginning. They say, "He/she is running scared before even getting started." "I could have told him it wouldn't work."

The truth is: To pray *before* **a venture shows wisdom** to discern our limitations. We are keenly aware of our lack of knowledge on our subject, so why "gamble" on the outcome? Time, effort, and money are costly investments which can be totally lost. So to pray **does not show weakness, but** *strength of character* that the outcome of our venture will not be failure.

2. Some people think that **prayer is an admission of** *failure.* Their opinion says, "You have already tried, ran into a stone wall, have no place to go, nor anyone to which you may turn." These people are often delighted to feel you have suffered total defeat, and they don't really believe your prayers will help anything, since they do not pray themselves.

The truth is: To pray is not admitting that one has already failed, but, is a defense against the possibility of future failure. Why close the gate *after* the horse has fled, that is --- unless you plan to put another horse in the barn? We pray because **we need an immunity from failure,** not because we have already failed. Therefore, our prayers are meant to be spiritual thrusts toward accomplishment. This leaves no place for failure.

3. Some people think **prayer is meant to be a substitute for hard work.** Their idea is: if one prays he can count on not having to work hard, nor undergo the anxieties that hard work brings. In fact, some people really think the "work part" of gaining success will be eliminated with a few "well placed prayers." This leaves them free to sail through reversals or slowdowns which most of us must endure.

The truth is: There is no substitute for hard work. And, there are no real personal accomplishments without work. Furthermore, work leads one to produce, and production brings one to **SUCCESS.** To my knowledge, prayer is no substitute for anything. By praying, we are not trying to get out of doing things but, we **are trying to eliminate useless motion.** We are "not leaning towards our own understanding, but we **are** acknowledging God's superiority, that He might direct our path."

Yes, we pray, seeking God's assurance that our efforts will not be in vain. Many mistakes are so devastating in nature that they cannot be undone, and in some cases, these mistakes **can lead to total failure.** Since we are not seeking failure, but *success,* our prayers to God are humble requests for His assurance that our work will not be futile because of our limited knowledge.

Therefore, we are **not submitting our work to the Lord,** but, we are **submitting ourselves to the Lord that our human abilities, ideas, research, preparations, and work will come together for good, because we love the Lord.** So, our prayers **tug at the heartstrings of our heavenly Father as a little child tugs at the coat tail of his human father.** We are *sure* to get His attention, so **our prayers will get results,** if we only believe.

Lastly, our FAITH, HOPE, AND LOVE, previously discussed, find their accomplishment in submission of self to our Maker. Prayer offered in sincerity, and with persistence reinforces our spiritual/Christian attitudes, and truly does **assure our success beyond a doubt.**

B. PRAYER FROM THE DIVINE POINT OF VIEW:

1. Be assured my friends: From the Divine point of view, **"Your Father knoweth what things ye have need of, before ye ask Him."** [*Matthew 6: 8b*].

How happy we should be to know that our Father is aware of our needs. Because of this awareness He begins to furnish most of our needs before we are even aware that He exists. The provision of food, shelter, clothing, and other necessities are automatically furnished at birth by parents or others who assume these responsibilities. In fact, God seems to provide **all our material needs** throughout life, although not requested by many, and not thanked by most. Yet, **spiritual needs seem to be dispensed primarily by request,** because they are of more value. Although spiritual needs are more important to man, many prefer to do without, and some actually *reject anything of a religious nature.*

God also knows the desires of our heart. He is aware of our **desire to SUCCEED,** and through prayers of faith we obtain our desires. Please be aware, **God does not award us success at the expense of someone else. Neither does God grant us success outside the framework of righteousness.** This means that a Holy God will not work within an immoral, illegal, unrealistic framework to bless us.

Sometimes desire may be selfish, lustful, covetous, or even revengeful. God does not reward inordinate desires, so even with prayer, *nothing good happens.*

When one prays with full awareness of his own limitations, the Lord seems to pity him. God's pity is more than sorrowful feelings towards us. His pity takes the form of compassionate sympathy which goes beyond our limitations. It is said, "Man's extremity becomes God's opportunity." How wonderful!!!

God is always able to provide, whether it be needs or desires. If a favor was requested of us, most of us would have to make preparation to provide that favor to our friend. However, when God receives a prayer request, he does not retire to a back room to stir a certain mixture of good things by which to bless us. He seems to have multiplied blessings in store just waiting for our call.

Through God, all things are possible. He can open doors of opportunity to us which have always been closed for various reasons. He can also close doors of adversity behind us which may threaten to undo all our good efforts. So SUCCESS does not really depend on our ability to perform, but on God's ability to **provide our needs and grant our desires** as we submit to Him in prayers of humble sincerity. Does this affect you? **YES!!!**

PRAYING FOR SUCCESS!

Not only does the Lord know our needs and desires, not only is He able to provide, but **God is also willing to perform.** As we interact with others in our daily work-a-day world, there is great awareness how much we must depend upon others to assist our efforts. In reality, **we are highly dependent on the cooperation of others** in various fields **to exercise their will to perform on our behalf.**

But problems arise when we discover that those upon whom we must depend may well be able to assist us, but may not be willing to do so because of various reasons. So, WHAT SHALL WE DO? Well, **we pray a lot,** since we can not afford to be defeated by the lethargy of others disinterested in our project.

So, as we continue to **exercise our human will, we also pray God to exercise His Spiritual Will on our behalf.** It is often uncanny how **the Lord can touch the heart of those who formerly refused us,** for the Divine Will is almost always exercised through others to provide our needs. However, He may elect to direct us to some place else and someone else. For **God's Will is always done in behalf of those who love Him.**

"Eye hath not seen, nor ear heard, neither have entered into the heart of man, the things which God hath prepared for them that love Him." [*I Corinthians 2: 9*]

Yes, positive *human* attitudes and positive *spiritual* attitudes **reinforced by submissive prayer borne on the wings of love,** seem to unlock the treasure house of heaven. God's blessings seem to flow freely to those who express their **LOVE** toward their Maker, and seek His direction in their **DRIVE TO BECOME SUCCESSFUL.**

TO YOU WHO ARE SEEKING TO BECOME SUCCESSFUL: *Are you still with me?* Then read on!!!

WE MUST SUCCEED!!! WE MUST HAVE THE ASSURANCE THAT OUR MENTAL, PHYSICAL, AND SPIRITUAL EFFORTS WILL PAY OFF!!! Since we have been discussing the element of prayer as a vital determinant in gaining SUCCESS, we would be **just taking a chance** if there was no assurance that **prayer does change things.** It has taken some people years of living, one disappointment after another, and failure after failure to realize the value of seeking spiritual direction **outside of self.** Those unproductive years have **driven many to do nothing now until Divine direction is sought.**

BUT TO MY YOUNG READERS: there is no reason for you to waste years of your life by using the *trial and error method* to accomplish your goals. **Time is precious. It will not wait on you. Once passed, time cannot be recalled. YOU NEED ASSURANCE RIGHT NOW THAT PRAYER DOES WORK!!!**

C. DOES GOD *ALWAYS* ANSWER PRAYER?

Since introducing *prayer as a key element* of becoming **SUCCESSFUL,** it is only natural that those who have not been inclined to pray, may have questions. This is not unusual, since there are "different strokes for different folks." By this, I mean, all people do not relish the same values. But, **I truly believe and practice each step** which has been outlined on these pages. In fact, **even now, I am praying that this book on SUCCESS will help you to BECOME SUCCESSFUL.**

There are some who have tried prayer to *some degree,* but have not realized or received the answer expected or hoped for. So, unanswered prayers can often discourage one from seeking help from above. There may be several reasons for unproductive prayers. Insincerity, lack of faith, or other improper attitudes could be the reason one's prayers go unanswered. Yet the question is valid: **DOES GOD ALWAYS ANSWER PRAYER?**

THE ANSWER IS YES!!! GOD ALWAYS ANSWERS PRAYER!!! Not always as expected, not always as we choose and hope for, and *sometimes we don't believe He answers at all.* But be assured my friend: GOD ALWAYS ANSWERS PRAYER IN A POSITIVE WAY.

HIS ANSWERS ARE POSITIVELY YES! or NO! or WAIT! [*II Cor. 1: 18-20*]

1. THE REASON GOD ANSWERS **YES** TO PRAYER:

a) Your blessings have already been prepared by God, just waiting for your request to be made.

b) Your prayer of faith has activated God's blessings, so there is no reason to withold them any longer.

c) You have prayed within the will of God, for what He desired you to have in the beginning.

d) Your prayers have not been totally for self-aggrandizement, but also for the benefit of society. Therefore, intercession for others is honored.

e) Love for us motivates God to bless us with **success.**

2. THE REASON GOD ANSWERS *NO* TO PRAYER:

a) You may have exhibited shallow faith or no faith in your prayer request.

b) Your prayer may be motivated by greed, pride, or other selfish desire.

c) **Respect and reverence for God may be lacking.** Since the Lord never forces blessings or success upon us, He will not be forced into blessing us either. **But remember who He is.**

d) Sometimes one may become so anxious to accomplish, that prayer becomes a **demand for action.** God does not work by demand, but by request. So prayers must be tempered by humility of spirit.

e) **God may have something better for you** than what you have requested. Since our knowledge is so limited, and our vision so obscured, we do not always know what we need. So mental limitations sometimes causes spiritual limitations.

f) The **gift would be harmful.** The tendency to ask for "things" rather than "values" if granted can be detrimental to us. So in His infinite wisdom, the Master always provides such things that we need, and most things that we desire *if* we can handle these blessings without disasterous results.

3. THE REASON GOD ANSWERS *WAIT* TO PRAYERS:

a) **The time is not right.** Our God is "timely," so He is never too early nor too late. His ways are not our ways, for we tend to race ahead, not knowing what lies adhead. Sometimes He must adjust a situation to conform to our needs. So God may not come when you call, but He is right on time.

b) The **heart and mind are not ready to receive.** We previously mentioned the necessity for right motives for seeking. We must be in harmony with spiritual values, so prayer may or may not change God, but prayer brings us into position to receive Him as well as what He gives us. So He waits for the change to take place.

c) **There is a spiritual lesson to be learned.** In relation to the last paragraph, we find that one may want the gift, but not want the Giver. This attitude demeans God and will surely delay (if not kill) one's chance of receiving anything until one learns **he cannot USE God.**

d) **Love for us can be God's prime reason for saying wait.** The total reasons or any one just discussed above should show the compassionate love God has for His people. To wait leads to patience, and in your patience possess ye your souls [*Lk. 22: 19*].

— Notes —

CHAPTER VI.

THE ASSURANCE OF BECOMING SUCCESSFUL.

Everything that we have discussed so far has been designed to *help you realize that* **YOU, TOO, CAN BE SUCCESSFUL!!!**

Repetition of ideas, words, and phrases, is not accidental nor an oversight, but have been used purposely to reinforce our thinking. **For as one thinketh in his heart, so is he:** [*Prov. 23:7*]. Our thoughts have all been positive because our intentions are positive, and positive intentions lead to positive actions on our part.

> LET EACH MAN THINK HIMSELF AN ACT OF GOD, HIS MIND A THOUGHT, HIS LIFE A BREATH OF GOD; AND LET EACH TRY, BY GREAT THOUGHTS AND GOOD DEEDS, TO SHOW THE MOST OF HEAVEN HE HATH IN HIM. — *P.J. Bailey*

Dear readers, SUCCESS DOES NOT COME BY ACCIDENT, and we ruled out any possibility of LUCK from the beginning of chapter 2 of our discussion. There are also some who think "If anything can go wrong, it will go wrong." However, by this time I know you have joined me in sharing the positive attitudes that BECOMING SUCCESSFUL is more than an idea, or several work related steps.

Certainly, the spiritual/Christian attitudes of faith, hope, and love are indispensable elements in our quest for success. Also, praying for success is a major determinant in reaching our goals. But even so ... Is this enough???

A. **YOUTH IN JUNIOR HIGH, SENIOR HIGH, AND COLLEGE STUDENTS** want an ASSURANCE now and in their future days that they can gain success as they join the labor force. They desire to be accepted by peers *now* and *some guarantee* of acceptance in *future society.* Most young people do not want to wade through the "trial and error" methods of yesteryear which the previous generation suffered.

Modern technology seems to be less tolerant of errors now than in the past era. Computerized control of machinery, solid state equipment, robots, high definition communication equipment, and new developments in scientific data are but a few reasons young people seem to want an assurance of survival for their future.

B. **MIDDLE AGED ADULTS ARE CONCERNED FOR THEIR FUTURE.** The failure of banks, Savings and Loan Associations, unexpected mergers of large companies, financial takeover of large companies by smaller ones, erratic actions of the stock markets in major countries, and the Federal monetary deficit of America have all combined to make life miserable for some middle aged citizens. Bankruptcies are at an "all time high," home and business foreclosures are prominent, and many of these adults have children in college.

The fact is: Many middle-aged adults are worried and would like **an assurance** that they will be able to make it to retirement. Some are wondering if "any Social Security money will be left" at their retirement. Others wonder if the economy will "drain off" their financial reserves, while others worry about erratic stock and bond markets. Present investments in Money Market accounts, Certificates of Deposit, GNMAs, and FNMAs are fluctuating greatly. So, the question is: What are **my chances of SUCCESSFUL survival** to and beyond my retirement years?

C. **MANY SENIOR CITIZENS ARE VERY CON-CERNED** about their future status of life due to limited income and less opportunity to earn. Some worry about the waning value of investments due to inflation, fluctuation of stocks and bonds, and the possibility of tax increases. At this particular time, some are concerned about Medicare increases, and the surtax proposal on enrollees of Part B.

To travel in a foreign country or take a boat cruise is a lifelong dream of some senior citizens, but fear has taken precedence over desire. No doubt, some are conveniently yielding to the aches and pain which seem to increase daily. So, taking that long desired trip, fixing up the old house, starting that new business venture, throwing that "big" birthday party, buying a new car, and other retirement plans have been "put on hold" until things get better.

The truth seems to be: **I don't know what's ahead.** What if I get sick? What will the "kids and grandkids" think? The price of everything has gotten so high. I don't really need that new car, that cruise, the house remodeled. If I bought new clothes or threw a big party, friends would say "I am showing off." A new venture would take too much out of me at my age, and ON, and ON, and ON. **NONSENSE!!!**

The fact is: *We older people do tend to worry too much.* And worry seems to be rooted in uncertainty of the future. So what we need is a greater measure of confidence in someone outside of self. Fear of becoming dependent on others does present an unpleasant prospect since we have always been so proud of our independence. Well, we *can* have a great measure of *assurance* that our life can be happy and filled with contentment in the future, **even at our age.** In reality, **at our age and with our past experiences, we should have already discovered the secret of abundant living.**

C. MANY SENIOR CITIZENS ARE VERY CONCERNED

One senior citizen gives this account of his life:

For years I felt sorry for myself as I worked a seven-day week. Then all too suddenly, my dependents were gone and on their own. The pressure eased, and I retired. Free at last! Now I could sleep late, go where I pleased, when I pleased.

But it didn't work out that way. Every morning I awoke to an empty calendar. I could putter, make do with little jobs around the house, and go grocery shopping. I tried to interest myself in hobbies, but some of us just aren't born to be hobbyists.

I began to suffer vague aches and pains. My dreams, curiously became angry dreams: I would wake up in the middle of the night with anger, and clenched fists. Mentally and physically, I felt washed up.

So I went back to work. The aches and pains gradually disappeared, the dreams sweetened. Today, at 71, I feel a sense of purpose and pride in my life that only work gives. In my experience, the hardest-working people always seem the happiest. Some people may enjoy their retirement years by doing nothing, and it's O.K. if that is what they want, but that's not for me. So, **my secret of abundant life is to keep on working, keep on producing, and keep on being happy in the process.**

HAPPINESS IS BEING PRODUCTIVE

D. **MANY PARENTS OF YOUNG CHILDREN ARE VERY CONCERNED FOR THEIR SUCCESS.** It is only natural for parents to want the best for their children. This concern signifies a strong love abiding within the heart of those parents and indicates the will to go to any lengths for their children. **You are to be commended** dear parents for that love, especially since the success of small or young children depends *directly upon the parents.*

Home training is the most important step in a youngster's life. The parent is the role model for small children and they grow up to believe the parent **is always right.** Usually up to the "teen" years, the child accepts everything that he has seen or heard in the home, since these are termed the "formative years." Therefore, what the parents do are of utmost importance during these years.

PARENTS OF TEENAGERS ARE VERY CONCERNED FOR THEIR SUCCESS!!! This also is the natural tendency of good parents. As their children grow to become teenagers, they have been exposed to influences from various sources and usually embraced many values not taught in the home. Young people in their teens also tend to become independent in thinking so that they question some parental values which have been established for them.

TEEN-AGERS ARE CON-CERNED FOR THEIR OWN SUCCESS!!! As observed in chapter I, Section D, Items 1-12, youth come to expect much from parents and from society. So they want to dis-cuss these desires and ex-pectations, not only with parents, but also with school teachers, counselors, peers, and sometimes with pas-tors. They **want to make good on their own.** And who's to say that they can not do it? However, they too, want ASSURANCE OF THEIR FUTURE SUCCESS IN LIFE.

COLLEGE STUDENTS ARE CONCERNED FOR THEIR OWN SUCCESS!!! Freshman students who are enrolled in Colleges or Universities out of City or State away from where home is located soon experience the trauma of a new environment and unfamiliar faces.

Since college life is much different from high-school life, and since parents are not so available, the Fresh-man must mature quickly in order to adapt to this new world. Because of his desire to SUCCEED, he soon learns to stand on his own feet, "bite the bullet," and turn his attention to getting the education that he seeks.

Students who attend college in their home town es-cape the trauma brought on by location change, but the new environment still poses a challenge to them. Even though still living at home where assurance of parental help is available, the Freshman wants a **concrete assurance** outside of the home that he can make it in college life. That ASSURANCE IS AVAIL-ABLE FROM THE RIGHT SOURCE.

E. YOU CAN INCREASE YOUR MENTAL POTEN-TIAL FOR SUCCESS.

Excerpts from an article by John Douglas published and copyrighted in November 1980 states the following:

The teenager had crushing news for his parents. Slow from infancy, troublesome in school, he was now capping his academic failures with a disgraceful expulsion order: "Your presence in class is disruptive and affects the other students."

Years later, he recalls his learning problems philosophically: "My intellectual development was retarded, as a result of which I began to wonder about space and time only when I had already grown up. Naturally, I could go deeper into the problem than a child." So, eleven years after expulsion from school, **young Albert Einstein** published the **Theory of Relativity** that changed our understanding of the universe.

No one in this century has been more widely recognized as a genius than Einstein. Yet his problems with early intellectual development and his peculiar gifts **cast great doubt on all our conventional ideas about genius, intelligence** or "I.Q." Einstein showed early defects in innate abilities, but aptitudes that he had learned rather than inherited were crucial to his genius.

Now, these powerful aspects of intelligence are getting close attention in a new wave of research. **A better understanding of these abilities is emerging from research along four major lines:**

1. Intellectual Quotient

I.Q. test scores are not as important as once believed. According to recent studies, I.Q. accounts for only about 35 to 45 percent of variation in students academic performances. Also, studies demonstrate that success in school may not be a guarantee of success in later life. However, experimental preschool programs have helped raise the scholastic ability of slum children, and some psychologists say that any healthy person can learn abstract reasoning skills.

2. Creativity

I.Q. scores which reflect on a single correct answer through logical steps, measure only about a half-dozen variables of mental ability. Tests which involve finding many solutions to a problem, measure only a few more variables. So, creativity if considered by itself, is just another aspect of intelligence, almost as narrow as I.Q.

3. Personality

Individuals who achieve greatness in some intellectual endeavor usually do so through force of personality as much as through sheer smartness. In the past, narrow definitions of intelligence usually excluded personality factors. Today, it has been discovered that people with great intellectual accomplishment differ from ordinary people in several personality traits. These traits are curiosity, persistence, and capacity for self-criticism — qualities that Einstein had. Also highly creative people show unusual open-ness, independence, imagination, and playfulness.

4. Brain structure and chemistry.

More knowledge of brain physiology may help us understand some other intellectual faculties not measured by I.Q., or creativity, or personality tests. The link between emotional involvement with a subject and one's ability to comprehend it appears to be a chemical "reward system" located in the brain. The emotions seem to reward the attention center for a job well done. This creates a feeling of satisfaction and well-being within the person.

The point is: **The majority of us excel in some facet of mental ability.** Some people are better than others at problem solving, others excel at originality, still others succeed at mental tasks which require persistence. **All of these traits are key components of human intelligence.**

To discover and develop your own intellect, ask yourself questions like these:

a) What do I like working with: words or numbers, abstract concepts or concrete ideas?

b) Am I better at dealing with people or things, and why?

c) When I'm explaining something, do I draw pictures, use words, or do I prefer to act things out?

d) Faced with a new situation, do I tend to memorize things or figure them out?

e) For fun, would I rather solve puzzles or make up stories?

f) Am I better at grasping the specific relationship between things or at seeing the whole picture?

g) Given a choice between two jobs, would I take the one demanding quick action or the one requiring patience?

Any combination of these diverse skills recognized, could help one to increase his mental potential for success. Thus the **secret is to realize that no one trait or ability is sufficient to accomplish your goal.**

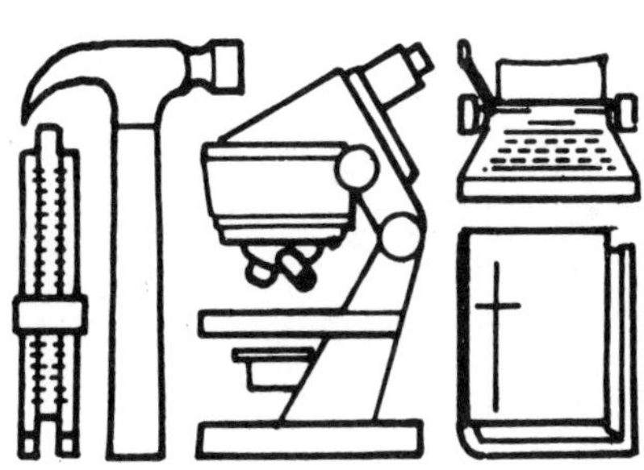

What do I really believe?
WILL GOD REALLY HELP ME???

CHAPTER VII.

HOW TO BE ASSURED OF BECOMING SUCCESSFUL.

A. **It seems that EVERYBODY wants to be successful.** *Pre-teen adolescents* want approval of parents, teachers, peers, and other adults. This desire for approval of others is a social desire that is saying: **"I want people to like me,** even as a child, I want others to respect me, and help me to *be somebody."* In other words, "I want to become SUCCESSFUL."

Teen-agers are trying to reason with parents, grandparents, or guardians by implying that values of the previous generation may not be adequate for today's society. Many teen-agers "run scared" because of the drug/alcohol problem in the schools and the community. Most "teens" want **no part** of this, even though some of their friends are caught up as users or pushers. These young people are looking ahead to becoming **morally successful** without degrading themselves by accepting low values of life. These young people want a MORAL ASSURANCE of SUCCESS.

College students and **young adults in the job market** want to be successful through college, apply their training and skills to earn an honest but decent living. They primarily seek monetary values that will enable them to purchase things considered necessary to *social and personal SUCCESS.* They want to be considered somebody as they climb the ladder to academic, and professional accomplishments — no holds barred. Young people in this age bracket like to feel that they "have what it takes" to make it in this world, YET, **the** shadow of possible failure hangs like the "Sword of Damocles" in the life of many. But ASSURANCE CAN BE YOURS as you seek fulfillment.

Middle-aged adults have usually been around long enough to become somewhat experienced in the affairs of life. You have probably accomplished much if not most of your goals in life. Yet, you may have **some discontentment** due to the routine followed year after year. Also since reaching some of your goals, monetary and social values have declined in importance. This fact **leaves a void in the life of many middle aged people.** You now discover a lack of **spiritual values** which have become vitally necessary to personal fulfill-ment. **Spiritual values** *will* provide the assurance you need for fulfillment.

Senior citizens, do not "sell yourselves short." At this time in your life, you should be the **most happy people alive.** Perhaps you have gained money and high social status. Perhaps you are much respected by friends and much loved by children, grandchildren, and other relatives. YET, YOU ARE NOT SPIRITU-ALLY FULFILLED. **That missing link must be supplied** if you will become COMPLETELY SUCCESSFUL. **THE ASSURANCE OF SPIRITUAL VALUES MUST BE ADDED TO YOUR LIFE.**

B. SHOOT FOR THE TOP OF THE SUCCESS LADDER.

Ambition seems to know no boundaries. Down through history many people have aspired to "go all the way" up the ladder of prosperity to become **Tycoons.**

A Tycoon [*Shogun in Japanese*] is the name given to one who reaches for and **attains the pinnacle of success** as a powerful, industrialist, financier, or magnate. And, of course, such power usually also brings wealth. But, what is so special about Tycoons?

Well, Tycoons may differ in many ways since they fill the spectrum from extroverted outgoing free-spenders to introverted tight-wad recluses. And yet, they do have many things in common that seem to be standard for those with great aspirations.

Those who shoot for the top of the **success ladder** are driven by a passion for work. Their work takes precedence over wives, children, vacations, and hobbies. They freely admit that they are "workaholics," even after having become wealthy to the point of fulfillment of all needs and desires.

Tycoons are often so intent on work that they look upon vacations as a waste of time, and at the least, a nuisance to be ignored. The Tycoon needs an extrordinary amount of energy to satisfy his passion for work, and regards a confession of fatique as an admission of weakness or a lack of dedication.

Does anything else motivate successful people to work so hard? YES! Money may draw people into business or entrepreneurship in the first place, but money is not usually the motivator that causes one to seek the "top of the heap." Then, **what IS the great motivator? POWER!!!**

Some top business people are quite frank about their addiction to the quest for power. For some, the position of power and influence is the greatest stimulation that they can experience for fulfillment and contentment.

Tycoons are extremely intelligent, persistent, and competitive with a compulsive curiosity. These traits show up early in their careers and remain a major part of their make-up. Even after reaching the top, the Tycoon remains obsessed with details. They are masterful opportunists, ever alert to any chances for personal advancement. They are tougher and more aggressive, yet, they ingratiate themselves with others on the way up.

Tycoons believe in their jobs, their products, the free enterprise system, and themselves. Lastly, **most Tycoons are spiritual minded and practice spiritual values.** Now, **DON'T YOU WANT TO SHOOT FOR THE TOP OF THE SUCCESS LADDER AND BECOME A TYCOON?**

MAKE SURE —
YOU'RE ON TARGET!

C. **THE ATTAINMENT OF SPIRITUAL VALUES ARE THE GREATEST ASSURANCE OF BECOMING SUCCESSFUL!!!**

"This book of the Law must ever be on your lips; you must keep it in mind day and night so that you may diligently observe all that is written in it. Then you will prosper and be successful in all that you do."

— Joshua 1:8 [New English Bible]

The people to whom these powerful words were written more than 3,440 years ago were nomads without a country of their own, without a home as shelter from the elements, and without fields to plow, plant, or harvest. These were the remnant of a People whom God had claimed as His own.

It may seem strange that the God who created the Universe, and who sustains it would have a people so destitute and bereft of what we call the bare necessities of life. There was no shortage of material goods, for God was able to provide their every need. He had proven this fact during the Exodus of His people from Egypt during an eighteen month period of travel enroute to their destination.

After their arrival, these travelers are camped outside the invisible gate of Canaan, the land which "flows with milk and honey." God had promised to his people a homeland through his servant Moses, but **because of unbelief,** the people were turned back to wander in the desert regions another forty years.

Now, a new generation of God's chosen have arrived at the same place to which their forefathers had previously been. Out of those original people, only Moses, Caleb, and Joshua have survived the 40 year trek. But now, God takes Moses to his heavenly home.

JOSHUA COMMANDING THE SUN
TO STAND STILL

"All things are possible to him that believeth." Mark 9:23.

GOD ALWAYS WANTS HIS PEOPLE TO BE SUCCESSFUL!!! So God renews His Covenant promise of a new homeland with Joshua and with this new generation through Joshua, Israel's new leader.

The Covenant was a reciprocating agreement whereby God's blessings would be lavishly given **if Joshua and the people would believe and remain faithful** to Him without reservation. Then Joshua was further commanded to **be strong and courageous, without fear or dismay** (spirit of failure). Through this admonition by the Lord, Joshua was **ASSURED that God would be with him wherever he would go** [*Joshua 1:9;* .

THAT POSITIVE ASSURANCE WAS ALL JOSHUA NEEDED. But take note: God was to be honored with a *spiritual faithfulness and obedience* **BEFORE JOSHUA'S SUCCESS WAS GUARANTEED.**

So, as Joshua was highly SUCCESSFUL, so can we be assured of great success as we allow God to lead us in everything.

D. **CHRISTIANS ARE ALWAYS SUCCESSFUL!!!**

This statement is made without any reservation on my part since I can easily remember when the rent was due and the cupboard was bare in our household. You shall be spared the sob story of my past life, but it is sufficient to say things needful have not always been available in our house.

Although "things" are not the most important items in life, the "absence of things needful to life" seem **very important** when they are not available. But, in due time the Lord opened **my spiritual eyes** to see *my true need was Christ Jesus.*

"First be eager to have God as your King, and all these things will come to you as a matter of course."
— *Matthew 6:33 [Beck and Phillips]*

"I am come that they might have life, and that they might have it more abundantly." — *John 10:10b [KJV]*

If you have already embraced God's Living Word and yielded yourself to the saving grace of Christ, then **you have already experienced the SUCCESS of the new birth.** FAITH, HOPE, AND LOVE are ATTITUDES which you practice on a daily basis as the natural result of living the Christian life. YOU ARE SOMEBODY ALREADY, so you should be fulfilled right now!

However, if there still seems to be a missing link in your bid for successful living, please **examine yourself** and engage in meditative prayer. I cannot tell you what the problem might be, but the Holy Spirit abides within, and He will SURELY open your understanding. Please remember: YOU ARE A CHILD OF THE KING, and it is His will that we LIVE A LIFE OF OVERFLOWING BLESSINGS.

My friend, if you are **one who lives on the fringe of Christianity,** you may not have experienced the success you are seeking because it is very likely that you have not followed the steps suggested to attain the success desired. **God wants you to have success,** but you must *first seek the kingdom of God and His righteousness.* Then, all these **things** [*elements of success*] will be given you in addition. Many people may be religious minded and embrace some religious values, but that is not enough. **The Kingdom of God is the rule of God in the heart of an individual,** so one should yield to His rule before seeking His blessings. Then, SUCCESS will surely become your blessing.

My dear seeker: you may be among those who "give no quarter and take no quarter" in religious matters. Perhaps yours is a scientific mind which has chosen to ignore the platitudes of religious speech as you pursue your goals of life. Or could it be that you simply do not believe in a God who would allow so many disastrous events to occur in our world?

You may believe that you are **"The master of your fate and the captain of your soul"** so that you need not accept nor follow a Christ who **may not be able to deliver.** Certainly, you have a right to your opinion, and the right to exclude anything from your life in which you do not believe. You may also have made certain accomplishments in life which you measure as SUCCESS. GOOD! But please take note my friend: **Gaining a measure of academic, industrial, monetary, athletic, artistic, or any other type success is no ASSURANCE that one is fulfilled.**

Religious values are real, they are here to stay, and cannot be carted off like an old car to the junk yard. For Christ, the Founder of Christianity thusly advises us who follow Him:

"A man can have only what God gives him." —
— *John 3:27* [*The New English Bible: New Testament*]

"For without me, you can do nothing at all."
— *John 15:5c* [*C.H. Rieu*]

Yes, my friend, all who will be SUCCESSFUL, will not, and **cannot find the full measure of their success within themselves apart from Christ Jesus.** Many have tried and some have even gained wealth from the world, only to realize that happiness and true contentment have eluded them. The way of the world is rough and rocky with many detours and pitfalls awaiting him who travels without the direction and guidance of a loving Christ. And although the Christian is *not promised immunity from trouble,* the Lord has promised He would always be with us.

"For God Himself has said, I will never forsake you, nor will I ever abandon you." — *Hebrews 13:5*
[*The Twentieth Century New Testament*]

What a tremendous promise! What a wonderful assurance we as Christians have of gaining the complete, unfailing, happy, success which leads to REAL CONTENTMENT. Our Saviour has paid the price to purchase our salvation, and only through the salvation which He offers can we be assured of our fulfillment. THIS ASSURANCE IS WHAT WE HAVE BEEN SEEKING ALL THE TIME!!!

**MONEY IS NOT A REAL MEASUREMENT OF SUCCESS,
BUT, IS A BY-PRODUCT OF
BECOMING SUCCESSFUL.**

SUMMARY OF CHAPTERS IV, V, VI, AND VII.

In order to reinforce what we have discovered in the past four chapters, we should observe that several things have been required to achieve the SUCCESS THAT BRINGS HAPPINESS:

1. DEVELOPING *RIGHT ATTITUDES* CAN MAKE US SUCCESSFUL.

2. WE SHOULD *PRAY TO GOD* TO BECOME SUCCESSFUL.

3. WE *CAN BE ASSURED* OF BECOMING SUCCESSFUL.

4. *HOW WE CAN BE ASSURED* OF BECOMING SUCCESSFUL.

RIGHT ATTITUDES:

Since we have quickly discovered that gaining success is more than a mechanical exercise, we are encouraged to develop the spiritual attitudes of FAITH, HOPE, AND LOVE. Even though one may not be spiritual-minded he is so limited in human ability and knowledge that right attitudes are indispensable if he will gain his desire.

FAITH along with its twin companion of work, is the key that opens the door of prosperity. Use of these twin companions is not a blind venture nor an exercise in futility, but is a positive step in attaining the goal that we seek.

The attitude of HOPE fosters patience, and patience leads to endurance to tolerate situations that we cannot regulate. God then regulates those conditions beyond our control while also regulating *our disposition* towards those situations. As our disposition is changed, we learn to persist in doing what we can do, and hope for that which we cannot yet see.

The attitude of LOVE a vital part of the formula for success. By definition, we *do not* believe the term "love" to be a catch-all phrase. The love we refer to is the greatest attibute derived from the heart of God, expressed through His Son Jesus, and fulfilled through the Holy Spirit.

Making the God of holiness the object of our love rather than the mammon of worldly possessions, elevates our desires for success to a spiritual level rather than a humanistic level. Therefore, our love is a reflection of God's love, and expresses our gratitude to Him, our concern for society, and our respect for co-workers as we pursue our goal.

PRAYING TO GOD:

Almost everyone can attest to the **potent persuasive power** of prayer and what it has and can accomplish. However, there are a **few** people who will not acknowledge any need to pray. Of course, **they are observing prayer from the human point of view.** Some think prayer is an admission of weakness and fear on one's part. In truth, **to pray before a venture shows wisdom** to discern limitations.

Some people think to pray is to admit failure. In truth, praying is a defense against the possibility of failure.

Some people think prayer is meant to be a substitute for hard work. In truth, prayer is not meant to eliminate work, but **to eliminate useless motion.**

In reality, **praying to God is submitting the self to God** that human effort will be reinforced by God's Spiritual Power.

From the Divine Point of View, prayers of the believer combine with his faith in God, his hope through God, and his love for God shows that humble submission, required to receive.

God is able to provide for us, whether it be for needs or desires. He can open doors of opportunity or close doors of adversity. God is also willing to perform in providing for us what we cannot provide for ourselves.

It is also very important to remember that **prayers are never in vain,** for God ALWAYS ANSWERS PRAYER IN A POSITIVE WAY. We may not always see the results of His answers, but please be assured, whatever the answers, they are **always for our benefit.** For God never gives anything artificial nor harmful to His people.
— *Matthew 7: 9, 10* [*Smith*]

DESIRE FOR ASSURANCE:

One should not expect success to come by accident nor by luck. **We want assurance that human ideas, preparations, and work will not be in vain.** In addition to human efforts, **we further expect our spiritual efforts to reinforce human efforts** to ASSURE OUR SUCCESS.

Young people in Junior High, Senior High, and College are desperate to accomplish their goals without delay and certainly without failure, since **you're only young once.**

Young adults and middle-aged adults are anxious for assurance that bank failures, financial takeovers, stock manipulations, and America's monetary deficit will not force them into bankruptcy. The drug problem, home mortgages, children in school, job security, and one eye on retirement are all reasons to desire positive assurance of economic stability in today's culture.

Many senior citizens and retirees also want assurance about their status of life. Being on a fixed income, fluctuations in investment values, and the possibility of **tax increases from various sources** all call for assurance of economic stability in their world.

Because of fear of the future, many "seniors" are afraid to invest any time, money, or effort **in their own future happiness. We want an ASSURANCE that present values will remain stable** that worry will *not consume us.*

HOW WE CAN BE ASSURED:

Honestly now, just who *can* give us *any measure of assurance* for the future? No person on earth can, for we **must walk by faith rather than by sight.** Children, teen-agers, college students, young adults, middle-aged adults, senior citizens, and all retirees are seeking the same thing. **WE WANT TO BE ASSURED OF GAINING SUCCESS WITH PEACE, PROSPERITY, HAPPINESS, AND FULFILLMENT THAT WILL BE PERMANENT.** That's all!!!

The **attainment of spiritual values are the greatest assurance of becoming successful.** In Old Testamental Biblical times Joshua experienced many victories over heathen enemies by committing himself to honor, believe in, and obey the God of Israel. In turn, Joshua was completely successful in the task of leading the Lord's people into the "promised land."

In New Testamental Biblical times it was a proven fact **that those who submitted to Christ Jesus as Saviour of the soul and Lord of the life had already experienced the success of the new birth.** Those who submit to Christ are called Christians, and **Christians are the most likely people to realize their goals of complete successfulness.**

CHAPTER VIII.

LOOKING AT OTHERS WHO HAVE BECOME SUCCESSFUL

A. SINCE BIBLICAL TIMES, history books are filled with SUCCESS STORIES of those who have made great accomplishments in life. From the period of Christian Beginnings (4 B.C. through the periods of Pagan Domination, Papal Domination, Western Reform, and through Rationalism and Secularism in A.D. 1648 to the present time, many Christians have lived, some have suffered, but all have succeeded in their service to God and society.

The Apostles, early Church Fathers such as Clement, Ignatius, Origen, Irenaeus, and Cy-

prian were successful.Augustine, Charlemagne, Thomas a'Kempis, Martin Luther, Zwingli, Calvin, and other Reformers have contributed much to society also.

As we move closer to modern times, we become aware of Thomas Jefferson, Roger Williams, John and Charles Wesley, Harry E. Fosdick, Karl Barth, D.L. Moody, George Truett,

George Washington, Abraham Lincoln, Caruso, Dickens, Edison, Firestone, Paderewski, Rockefeller, Roosevelt, and others who were highly successful, and many of whom were great Christians.

Some other people who have been considered highly successful, and who lived in the 19th or 20th century are as follows:

Frederick Douglass, (1817-1895) a former slave rose to become the first Black in America to serve as U.S. Marshall; Recorder of Deeds; Bank president; Journalist and Lecturer. In 1847, he founded the "North Star" newspaper.

Frederick Douglass
(1817-1895)

George Washington Carver, (1864-1943) born of a slave mother, became one of the greatest Agricultural Scientist of all times. He was also an accomplished pianist. In 1973, he was elected to the Hall of Fame of great Americans.

Joel E. Spingarn became a Columbia University Professor and distinguished literary critics. In 1914, he instituted the "Springarn Gold Medal" which is now given annually for the "Highest or Noblest Achievement by an American Black."

Duke Ellington

Duke Ellington, (1899-1974) writer of over 2,000 songs, rose to the top of the music world through his creative ability. He was a rare combination of composer, arranger, and band leader. Although he never finished high school, he received ten honorary Doctorate degrees. He was honored by four U.S. Presidents, Pope Pius XII, Queen Elizabeth of England, and received the French Legion of Honor.

Ralph J. Bunche, (1904-1971) was a graduate of U.C.L.A. with Phi Beta Kappa honors. With a Masters from Harvard University, he taught Political Science at Howard University. After receiving a Ph.D from Harvard, Dr. Bunche became the first Black official to serve in the State Department. Later, he served as Mediator at the United Nations, and was the first Black to be awarded the Nobel Peace Prize. Bunche later became Under Secretary of the U.N.

Dr. Bunche

Thurgood Marshall, the grandson of a former slave, graduated from Lincoln University, Cum Laude in 1929. He graduated from Howard's Law School, Magna Cum Laude, and was later appointed Judge of the U.S. Circuit Court of Appeals (N.Y.) in 1961; U.S. Solicitor General in 1965; and the first Black U.S. Supreme Court Justice in 1967.

Thurgood Marshall

Martin Luther King, Jr. (1929-1968) was a brilliant leader who advocated non-violence against racial, economic and educational prejudice. He entered Morehouse College at age 15. After graduating from Morehouse with an A.B. and Crozer Theological Seminary with a B.D., King earned a Ph.D. degree from Boston University. A co-pastor with his father of Ebenezer Baptist Church in Atlanta, Ga., Dr. King was the recipient of many awards. At the age of 35, Dr. King was the youngest person ever to win the Nobel Peace Prize in 1964, then donated the prize money of $54,000 to the civil rights movement.

M. L. King

William (Bill) Cosby, has been highly successful in the field of entertainment as a comedian, actor, writer, and producer. He is the first Black T.V. actor to receive an Emmy award for the best continuance performance by an actor in a dramatic series.

"Bill" was a high school dropout, who later earned his high school diploma and a B.A. degree through correspondence. Bill also earned a Ph.D. in education from the University of Mass. Dr. Cosby has also earned another 3 Emmys and 6 Grammy awards. He also has given millions to various colleges.

Bill Cosby

Alex Haley, is the Pulitzer Prize winning author of "Roots." Inspired by his grandmother's stories of slave times, Haley's best-selling book took 12 years to research and write. Although a college drop-out, he joined the Coast Guard and later retired as Chief Journalist. He has written freelance for top magazines, and has also been awarded the Spingarn Medal.

Alex Haley

B. Some people whom I have personally known as successful persons in the State of Oklahoma are further listed:

Inman E. Page, an able educator, became the first president of the Agricultural and Normal University at Langston, Oklahoma in 1897. This institution was later called Langston University. Professor Page later served a number of years as Principal of Douglass High School in Oklahoma City, Okla.

Thomas Cox Allen, (1907-1989) is one of the first black aviators to fly coast to coast some 50 years ago. In January 1989, a British made movie was released which tells of the adventures of two black pilots, (Allen and J. Herman Banning) as they sky hopped across the United States. The movie was based on a book written by Allen.

Mr. Allen received the Distinguished American Citizen award from the United States Air Force, and the Patrick Henry Patriotism Medal from the Military Order of the World Wars. He has also been inducted into the Oklahoma Afro-American Hall of Fame.

During the last ten years of his life, Mr. Allen spoke before countless Freedom Forums, and Youth Citizenship Seminars, conducted by the American Citizenship Center for high school students in Oklahoma, Texas, Kansas, Missouri, and Alabama. He also lectured often at the Air Space Museum at the Kirkpatrick Center in Oklahoma City.

Roscoe Dungee was born the son of a Baptist minister, who was a former slave. His father died in 1902 leaving a library of 1500 books to the family. Through these books, Roscoe's life was enriched.

Roscoe learned about printing at Langston University and having written for a number of newspapers, he launched his own newspaper in 1915. This newspaper was called the **Black Dispatch,** which was soon circulaing nation wide. Mr. Dungee was for many years a civil rights leader, and held a number of positions of distinction.

Tom Allen, one of the first black aviators to fly coast to coast, stands with an exhibit honoring his achievements at the Oklahoma Air Space Museum in Oklahoma City.

Amos T. Hall, a prominent attorney in Tulsa, Okla. was the first elected black judge in the State of Oklahoma, when he won out over three opponents in 1970. Mr. Hall was also prominently known as the Honorable Grand Master of the Most Worshipful Prince Hall Grand Lodge, F. & A.M. Jurisdiction of Oklahoma.

Hannah Diggs Atkins received her B.S. Degree from St. Augustine's College in Raleigh, No. Carolina. She received her Bachelor of Library Science Degree from the University of Chicago. She also has done additional study at the University of Oklahoma and the School of Law at Oklahoma City University.

Mrs. Atkins, wife of the late Dr. Charles N. Atkins who was a prominent Oklahoma City Physician, has many accomplishments to her credit. Mrs. Atkins became a member of the Oklahoma State House of Representatives in 1968, has served as an assistant director of the Department of Human Services of Oklahoma, and is presently serving as Oklahoma Secretary of State.

Hannah D. Atkins

Reverend Walter Kinsley Jackson was the seventh of twelve children born to Eddie and Adelaide Jackson. Arriving from the State of Georgia, the Jackson family settled in a rural area near Boley, Oklahoma, where at age 15, Walter began his preaching career. Reverend Jackson graduated from Bishop College, Dallas, Texas in 1937, married Miss Eula Lee Wilhite, and became pastor of the Corinth Baptist Church in Ardmore, Okla.

In 1945, Reverend Jackson came to the St. John Missionary Baptist Church of Oklahoma City as co-pastor with the Reverend John Wesley Johnson. Pastor Jackson later received the Doctor of Divinity Degree from Morris-Booker Memorial College in Dermont, Arkansas, and the honorary D.D. Degree from the Oklahoma School of Religion, Langston, Oklahoma. He has done additional study at Union Theological Seminary in Manhattan, New York.

PASTOR W. K. JACKSON

Dr. Jackson served 15 years as Executive Secretary Treasurer and 4 years as President of the Oklahoma Baptist State Convention. He also served as President of the Progressive Oklahoma Baptist State Convention. He has served numerous other positions and has received numerous awards for meritorious services.

In 1979 Dr. Jackson lead the St. John Church into a multimillion dollar facility. Church growth was tremendous with membership in excess of 2,000 persons.

In 1987, Dr. Jackson along with his co-pastor built a new wing to the previous structure, called "The Family Life Center." The new facility accommodates the gymnasium, library, nursery, administrative offices, and youth ministries classrooms. As of this writing, Dr. Jackson and the "Church" has just celebrated his "Sixty Years of Living, Loving, Leading, and Serving" in the Gospel Ministry. Forty-four of those years have been spent as Pastor of this the "Lord's Church."

Dear friends: there are many more names of prominent and not so prominent people who could be mentioned here as having attained great SUCCESS in their lifetime. Out of the fifteen short biographies given, most had many things in common:

• Most, if not all came from humble beginnings.
• Most, if not all had ambitions to accomplish.
• Most, if not all sought to serve society.
• Most, if not all overcame the odds through persistence.
• Most, if not all had spiritual convictions towards God.
• Most, if not all found happiness and contentment in life.

C. TRUST GOD TO GET CAREER ON RIGHT TRACT: — *Billy Graham*

DEAR DR. GRAHAM: I got out of school only a couple of months ago, but I am becoming very discouraged because I can't find a job. Maybe I trained for the wrong career. Please pray for me that somehow I will find the right place. **—R.M.**

DEAR R.M.: The most important thing I can tell you is that God has a perfect plan for your life---including your career. Your problem therefore, is not so much to find a job — but to find God's Will. Have you ever realized this, and are you asking Him to guide you to the right position?

You see, God is concerned about every detail of our lives because He loves us. He also wants to guide us if we will let Him.

"Good and upright is the Lord ... He guides the humble in what is right and teaches them His way" [*Psalm 25: 8-9*]. You only will be truly satisfied and at peace when you know you are in God's Will.

How do you discover God's Will in this situation? Begin by committing your whole life to Jesus Christ, trusting Him as your Savior and determining to obey Him as Lord of your life. Then make this question a matter of daily prayer, and ask God to guide you as you make decisions about your future.

How will He guide you? At times, He may open a door of opportunity that is clearly His Will. At times, He may give you as inner sense of assurance that a certain way is right for you. At times, He may even use others to help you evaluate your abilities and direct you. He may, for example, want you to get more education so you can sharpen the abilities He has given you.

So don't get discouraged but let this be a time when you love more of what it means to trust God.

God's promise is clear: "Trust in the Lord with all your heart ... and He will make your paths straight" [*Proverbs 3: 5-6*].   **— Tribune Media Services**

D. HOW TO KNOW THAT YOU ARE SUCCESSFUL!!!

You are successful: When you have given Christ your soul for salvation, your life for service, and your love in gratitude.

You are successful: When you have produced and given more to society than you have consumed and taken from society.

You are successful: When you have accepted all people at face value with equal respect and consideration.

You are successful: When you can love family, friends, and enemies with equal compassion.

You are successful: When you are at peace with the world, regardless to turmoil in the world.

You are successful: When you can stand tall with dignity and integrity, after having honestly done your best.

You are successful: When you can feel great contentment and fulfillment in life, with no remorse nor regrets.

**CONGRATULATIONS!!!
YOU HAVE BECOME SUCCESSFUL!!!**

KNOWING THAT YOU ARE SUCCESSFUL!!!

THAT MAN
IS A SUCCESS

Who has lived well
    Laughed often and loved much;

Who has gained the respect
    Of intelligent men
        And the love of children;

Who has filled his niche
    And accomplished his task;

Who leaves the world better
    Than he found it,
        Whether by an improved poppy,
        A perfect poem
            Or rescued soul;

Who never lacked appreciation
    of earth's beauty
        Or failed to express it;

Who looked for the best in others
    And gave the best he had.

— Author Unknown.

BIBLIOGRAPHY

Allen, Thomas Cox — As told by Mrs. Hannah Allen 1989

Atkins, Charles and Hannah
Dungee, Roscoe
Hall, Amos T.
Page, Inman E. — BLACK HERITAGE OF OKLAHOMA,
by Gene Aldrich, ©1973
by Thompson Book & Supply
Edmond, Oklahoma
By Permission

Bunche, Ralph J.
Carver, George W.
Cosby, William H.
Douglass, Frederick
Ellington, Duke
Haley, Alex
Spingarn, Joel E. — From INTERESTING PEOPLE:
BLACK AMERICAN HISTORY MAKERS,
©1989 by George L. Lee
By permission of McFarlane & Company, Inc.,
Publishers, Jefferson, N.C.

King, Martin L.
Marshall, Thurgood — Jet, ©1968 by Johnson Publishing
Co., Chicago, Ill.

Graham, Billy — Tribune Media Services, 1989
Orlando, Florida

Jackson, Walter Kinsley — TRIBUTE TO A FRIEND,
By Morris A. Curry, Sr. 1988

Kendall, Eugene — FUTURE IN YOUR HANDS,
A Letter to The Editor
Oklahoman & Times 1989

BIBLIOGRAPHY

Excerpts for Success Relates To Happiness — HAPPY PEOPLE: By Jonathan L. Freedman, Copyr. 1978

Excerpts for Seven Steps That Lead To Peak Performance — SECRETS OF PEAK PERFORMANCE: By Morton Hunt, Copyr. 1982 Reader's Digest

Excerpts for You Can Increase Your Mental Potential For Success — HOW TO INCREASE YOUR MENTAL POTENTIAL: By John H. Douglas, Copyr. 1980

AUTHORS OF QUOTATIONS USED

Bailey, P.T.
Beecher, Henry Ward
Emerson, Ralph Waldo
Herbert, George
Longfellow, Henry W.
Luther, Martin
Palmer, Gretta
Pliny, The Elder
Seneca
Smiles, Samuel
Steward, George David
Ulman, Samuel

SCRIPTURE QUOTATIONS USED

King James Version
Twentieth Century New Testament
The New Testament (James Moffatt)
Epistles Of Paul (W.J. Conybeare)
N.T. in Modern English, (J.B. Phillips)
N.T. (Ronald Knox)
Book of Acts (E.V. Rieu)

Text set in 12 point Helios Type
by Alpha-Omega Typesetting Service
Oklahoma City, Oklahoma